A STAFF TO THE PILGRIM

Ita

Cuthbert

Melangell

Gwenfrewi

Hilda

Aidan

Brigid

Brendan

David

A Staff to the Pilgrim

MEDITATIONS ON THE WAY
WITH NINE CELTIC SAINTS

Gabriel Cooper Rochelle

Foreword by Wally Swist

Illustrations by Michael S. Sayre

Golden Alley Press
Emmaus, Pennsylvania

Golden Alley Press
37 South 6th Street
Emmaus, Pennsylvania 18049

www.goldenalleypress.com

Golden Alley Press books may be purchased for educational, business, or sales promotional use. For information please contact the publisher.

Printed in the United States of America

3 5 7 9 10 8 6 4 2

A Staff to the Pilgrim: Meditations on the Way with Nine Celtic Saints
Gabriel Cooper Rochelle. -1st ed.

ISBN 978-0-9895265-6-2 print
ISBN 978-0-9895265-7-9 eBook

Illustrations © Michael S. Sayre

*Front cover: 'pilgrim' in composite illustration,
author Jose Antonio Alba, source www.pixabay.com, (CC0)*

Back cover photograph of the author © Emily Scott

Cover design by Michael Sayre

To Susan, my partner in love and life and faith.

Arglwydd, arwain trwy'r anialwch,
Fi, bererin gwael ei wedd.
Nad oes ynof nerth na bywyd
Fel yn gorwedd ny y bedd:
Hollaluog, Hollaluog,
Ydyw'r Un a'm cwyd i'r lan,
Ydyw'r Un a'm cwyd i'r lan.

Guide me, O thou great Redeemer,
Pilgrim through this barren land;
I am weak, but thou art mighty;
Hold me with thy powerful hand;
Bread of heaven,
Feed me now and evermore,
Feed me now and evermore.

Contents

FOREWORD

I first met Fr Gabriel in New Haven forty years ago, when he was a campus minister at Yale.

We would meet every Monday morning in the front office of the brownstone he and his family lived in. Lined floor to ceiling with shelves of books, the room faced the sidewalk on High Street. Our conversations were as nourishing as the bread and pasta Fr Gabriel made for family dinners, to which I was often invited. These were conversations of magnitude and depth, as we discussed poetry and spirituality from Wendell Berry to Tomas Transtromer, from Thich Nhat Hanh to Henri Nouwen. We talked of *The Practice of the Presence of God* by Brother Lawrence and the Jesus prayer.

These Monday conversations were springboards to transcendent moments in which the air filled with the intensity of a psychic pointillism. They offered me both clarity and a new vision, which would provide me with grist for thought and contemplation during the rest of the week. My initial source and first taste of discovering the numinous in the commonplace, the main thing I strive for in my poetic practice, may well have come from that book-lined front room. As Fr Gabriel writes in the meditation after the life of St Melangell in this volume, "to see the holy in the ordinary, the transcendent in the momentary, vast infinity within the confines of place…this is sometimes called seeing 'the cosmic Christ.'"

I am drawn to the rigorous philosophical investigation of the practice of maintaining an actual spiritual life as laid out in *A Staff to the Pilgrim*. Fr Gabriel gives an historical recounting of each of the nine saints, and each one serves as a touchstone for his meditative, and sometimes lyrical, extrapolations to help us in our spiritual practices of paying attention to one's inner voice, the practice of presence, and finding guidance in our lives. His discussion of *hiraeth* as spiritual mystery, or nostalgia, draws me in as I am drawn to Federico Garcia Lorca's literary trope of Duende, or mysterious spirit.

I found in Fr Gabriel's book parallels and complements to other works of spirituality that have nourished me over the years, both in philosophy and the quality of the craft of the writing itself. In his meditation upon the life of St Cuthbert, Fr Gabriel offers that "quiet is the threshold, not the doorway, but there can be no door without the threshold." This brings to mind the small book that offers large dimensions, Thomas Merton's *Thoughts in Solitude*.

In portraying St Brigid in her spiritual valor, reminding us that "anyone without a soul friend is like a body without a head," Fr Gabriel also befriends each of us. He befriends us by offering us spiritual guidance on our way to real healing. There is nothing about the path that is not *de rigueur*, since it is distinguished by integrity, and it is beyond anger, beyond coldness in others.

As Fr Gabriel writes, "the allure of the divine" is "beckoning us toward fulfillment." To me, this echoes with tones resonant in the poetry of Rainer Maria Rilke. As the eminent translator Stephen Mitchell writes of Rilke in conjunction with his composition of the *Sonnets to Orpheus*, he suggests that at first he was writing about Orpheus; at the end of the sequence he, himself, became Orpheus. The same can be said about Fr Gabriel – we move with him as he discusses the saints with us, then he graciously hands us our own staff to be pilgrims on our way.

Even in those long-ago Yale years, Fr Gabriel's interests lay in baking, calligraphy, and bicycling. It is a pleasure to recognize these three enduring threads interwoven in the tapestry of *A Staff to the Pilgrim*. We read about Fr Gabriel's encounter with the famous French bread baker, Lionel Poilâne, for whom bread was the heart of his spiritual vision. I recall Fr Gabriel's passion for the craft of calligraphy and our sharing a reverence for the work of Frederick Franck, whose spiritual ethos informed what was then a recent book, *The Zen of Seeing*.

My friend's zeal for bicycling continues to lead him to explore the spiritual presence therein. Reminiscent of Robert M. Pirsig's ontological explorations in *Zen and the Art of Motorcycle Maintenance*, Fr Gabriel tells us, "God is waiting if only we don't hold back and try to hold on to whatever has already gone by." That may be the mantra of the universal bicyclist, breezing on through the wind, sweeping past the countryside on physical and spiritual aerodynamics as both sacred exercise and devotional practice.

A Staff to the Pilgrim is iconic, inspirational, and provident in its offering of guidance for all of us in leading an active spiritual life. It offers us the beneficent combination of erudition and wonder – as in awe – with which it springs forth. When we are provided with a new and fruitful way of leading our lives in the world that combines the material and the physical with the spiritual and the transcendent, we are given an auspicious and true gift – a gift which this book marvelously makes to readers everywhere.

Wally Swist
South Amherst, Massachusetts
May 2016

ACKNOWLEDGMENTS

Many people were on the pathway that led to this book. My interest in matters Celtic goes back so many years it is impossible to trace or remember all the footfalls, but they include family members who walked in front of me. I am especially indebted to my parents who read folk tales to me in my childhood, thus instilling a love for folklore, especially Celtic material, in my soul.

I have learned from a host of contemporary writers and teachers, especially David Adam, A. M. Allchin, Jane Cartwright, David Jones, J. Philip Newell, John O'Donoghue, Edward Sellner, Ray Simpson. Thanks to Esther de Waal, who introduced many of us to the verses of the *Carmina Gadelica*. Those verses are often on my mind, as are the melodies and lyrics of the many great Irish and Welsh hymns with which I grew up. Thanks to Bill Cohea, dreamer and doer, who has provided many people and dogs with a spiritual oasis in Columcille, near Bangor, Pennsylvania. Thanks to the poet Wally Swist for eagerly accepting an invitation to write a foreword. My profuse thanks to Nancy and Michael Sayre, friends who believed in the project before I did.

INTRODUCTION

How we got on the path in the first place

Raise an inquisitive boy in Philadelphia, and he will wonder about the strange-sounding names of towns ringing round the area: Gwynedd, Bala Cynwyd, Bryn Mawr, Bryn Athyn, Bangor and Pen Argyl, and the melodic-sounding Nant-y-glo. Soon he is asking, where did all this Welshness come from? And not only Welshness, but also the Irish and Scottish influence that was everywhere, including the neighborhood Irishman's Tap.

My family has extended Celtic roots, so from childhood on I reveled in the tales of King Arthur, Sir Gawain and the Green Knight, the Tain, and the Mabinogion. I sensed something special and unique about the Celtic realm. These tales led directly into my life-long exploration of Celtic Christian spirituality, with its uniqueness and special qualities.

The Birth of Celtic Christianity

Christianity, like its parent religion Judaism, began on eastern soil. The cradle for these faiths stretched from Israel north into what is now Turkey, south into Egypt, and then east into the land between the rivers Tigris and Euphrates.

The faith of the early church moved west steadily from the beginning, sometimes brought by missionaries, sometimes carried in the knapsacks of Roman soldiers who, when mustered out of the army, often settled where they were released. In most cases, Christianity moved west without violence or imposition. By the end of the 2nd century, the church was already prominent as far west as what are now France and England. This was a remarkable achievement by any reckoning.

How did the church expand so quickly? One legend is that Joseph of Arimathea, who took the body of Jesus down from the cross and buried it in his own tomb, was a well-to-do tin merchant who traveled the Mediterranean basin west to the British Isles. He is also reputed to have been the uncle of Jesus and to have taken the boy with him on journeys – hence the tradition that the child Christ trod on English soil before his ministry began, as the poet William Blake wrote.

Legends aside, the early writer Tertullian (155-222) tells us that Christianity had made it to Britain during his lifetime. Eusebius (260-340), a thorough historian for his age, also wrote that Christianity had been long established in the British Isles. The Irish embraced Christianity before the time of St Patrick, who actually represents the second wave of Christian influence in Ireland.

Very early on, the Christian faith had grown into a comprehensive philosophy, which is surely part of the reason for its quick expansion even in times of persecution. Already by the second century, writers like Irenaeus and Justin Martyr were communicating that Christianity offered new and better ideas beyond the limited scope of religion at that time. Faith joined to intelligence overturned superstition and prejudice. The Celts became instrumental in this movement throughout the centuries, preserving and shaping it through the monastic tradition and local support for a spirituality tied to both hearth and church.

The Celtic understanding of martyrdom developed more fully than a sole focus on martyrdom-unto-death. This understanding also influenced the spread of Christianity westward. The Celtic church counted three kinds of martyrdom: white, green, and red. Red martyrdom was the witness that led to death, giving up one's life for the faith. Green martyrdom (sometimes called blue), accessible to all Christians, comprised the daily struggle for goodness and compassion by shedding bad habits, routines, and morals that separate us from God. White martyrdom meant to spend one's life for the faith by traveling on mission.

This full concept of martyrdom gave rise to extraordinary efforts by Christians from the British Isles. Sts Brendan and Columbanus are wonderful examples of those who left home to spread the faith. Once it reached the western boundary of the world, the Atlantic Ocean, it bounced back, more fully equipped, to parts of Europe not previously visited. The Celtic pioneers then traveled back into Europe, to France, Italy, and beyond, bringing with them a vision of church as a total way of life and a complete approach to thought. The main engine for these efforts was education, and the main vehicle was the monastery.

And so we come, after many a path taken, to this book.

Which Saints to Choose

Looking over the list of saints herein you will note, first, that we bypassed hundreds who could have been mentioned. Of necessity we chose a sampling of those whom we felt to be exemplars of a particular quality. The list is intensely personal and, to some small degree, arbitrary. Those who are familiar with the Celtic realm of Christian spirituality and faith might have chosen others. We do not mention St Columba, St Kentigern, St Colman, or St Patrick. So it goes; no slight is meant by their absence.

Every saint exhibits more than one quality; in fact, most of them exhibit *all* of the qualities we have chosen to meditate upon. For every look at, for instance, St Brendan and his burning desire for mission, we could just as easily look to him as a person filled with the Holy Spirit. For every look at St Melangell in her solitude, we could also look to her in her silence. For every instance of a saint whose tie to place is beyond the merely geographical, like St Gwenfrewi, we could have easily mentioned St David and his tenacious spiritual connection to several places in Wales.

The devotions themselves stray as well; we have put them in categories that made sense to us as we compiled the resource you have in your hands. Here again, that does not mean they could not have been perceived under another head. In matters of spirituality, everything is related to everything else. The peculiar and unique kind of spirituality that arose among Celtic peoples, particularly those of Wales and Ireland, is not limited to those lands (silence, solitude, Spirit: these things are *universally* regarded among Christians). Nonetheless, the composite picture seems to be uniquely characteristic of those locales. And beginning with the letter 's', the character traits lent assonance to our chapter titles.

The Missing S: Song

What is missing from our list is the 's' of song. Is this a virtue? Perhaps. Among the Welsh it was certainly so, particularly in the tradition of the Eisteddfod, the national poetry and song contests known to this day. The tradition of hymnody among the Welsh excels above all others, and there are notable Irish hymn tunes that will continue to stand the test of time. Sung or spoken, at the heart of Celtic spirituality is praise of the Blessed Holy Trinity; it shines through in any examination of the Celtic saints. The liturgy of the Celtic churches was noteworthy for the choral tradition, which likely flowed into Celtic lands by way of Gaul (France) and, ultimately, the Eastern Orthodox Church[1]. Hymnody has the ability to bind people together in community, and hence it was and remains a handmaiden to the Eucharist, particularly in the Celtic regions.

The Totality of Celtic Spirituality

We are doing something in this book which should not be done but which, unfortunately, must be done. What *should* be done is that we become immersed in the totality of Celtic Christian spirituality. Unfortunately, because we cannot communicate totalities, we are forced to break up a whole experience

---

1   This was examined over a century ago by F. E. Warren in his classic study of Celtic liturgy, *The Liturgy and Ritual of the Celtic Church*.

into its constituent parts. We are stuck with this problem in so many areas of our lives, and it is no less true with regard to Celtic spirituality.

Not only that, but it is almost impossible to communicate the air, the tenor, the sensibility, and the feeling of Celtic Christianity. It is like learning a language; you are best off being immersed in it rather than talking about it. Our approach to God is much the same, when we think about it; we are so much better off resting in God than talking about God.

Thus we are given a twofold problem: first, the impossibility of communicating a whole experience; and second, the practical problem that the inner music of Celtic Christian spirituality may have been so lost or forgotten that we may be called to re-creation before immersion.

Three Thoughts as We Walk Forward

Nevertheless, we are drawn forward. So please remember three points as you walk this meditative pathway.

First, and to repeat, everything is related to everything else. Though we may be talking about silence in a particular meditation, hidden within that aspect of spirituality will also be our sense of the presence of the Holy Spirit, our attempt to live simply, and the solitude that the silence enables. They are all interconnected.

Second, Christ is the heart and center of all Celtic Christian spirituality, whether his name is spoken, or hidden below the surface of the words. St Patrick's breastplate comes to mind, with its concluding *caim* (encircling prayer):

Christ with me, Christ before me, Christ
  behind me,
Christ in me, Christ beneath me, Christ above me,
Christ on my right, Christ on my left,
Christ when I lie down, Christ when I sit down,
  Christ when I arise,
Christ in the heart of every man who thinks of me,
Christ in the mouth of every one who speaks of me,
Christ in the eye of everyone that sees me,
Christ in the ear of everyone that hears me.

Third, hold in your heart the saint whom we propose as the key figure for each of the virtues. There is a prayer associated with each saint. Wrap it around the meditation as you read. Pray with and through that saint as you move along. May that road to and in the Spirit rise up to meet you.

A Note on Celtic Women Saints

Three things must be said about the women saints of Celtic lands.

First, strong women appear in both the history and the tales that precede the writings of the saints. There is the historical legend of the great Queen Boudicca, one of the last leaders of Celtic tribes to make a stand against the onslaught of the Romans. In folk tales, we think of Deirdre of the Sorrows, Brigid the goddess from the Irish tales, or Rhiannon and Branwen from the Mabinogion. Rhiannon is both wittier and stronger than her male counterpart, and Branwen's tragic life is limned in a way that casts her as a sympathetic character.

Secondly, though they appear throughout history, the number of women available for veneration or legend is far fewer than the number of men. This is a simple fact of history, for there were fewer women's monasteries in Ireland, Wales, and Northumberland than there were monasteries for men. The pool of contenders for hagiography is smaller; the list of women saints is concomitantly so.

Third, as has been pointed out by scholars of early saints' stories, women were not in charge of their own biographies at this point in history. Not until the 12th century do we begin to find women like Hildegard of Bingen, a powerful and wise leader of a monastic settlement whose wisdom carried her into the halls of the pope. In Britain we find Julian of Norwich, a legendary director of souls, who wrote her own story in terms of the "showings" or revelations that were given to her. Certainly a figure like Hilda of Whitby, abbess of a double monastery with houses for both men and women, ranks as a powerful saint in the earlier period. Even so, she was not in charge of her own story.

Thus, it is a fact of history that the writing of the stories of women saints depended upon men who were willing and able to valorize them for the general public. This is true for the women saints included in this book, for Ita, Melangell, Gwenfrewi, Hilda, and Brigid. We have given them over half of the book in a field in which they were, initially, a decided minority.

Because these saints are Celtic women, strength of character shines through even those stories that were controlled by men. Each of the women saints began as a beautiful young woman; their hagiographers have them spurning lovers to become lovers of Christ in a monastic setting. Gwenfrewi offers an extreme example, as she must survive death to make her way as an independent figure. And even her death must be overturned by male intervention. This is stock presentation; we will never be able to get beyond the hagiography as presented in that age to what we would, today, consider biography. However, if we are willing to take the time to study them, we can see through the finished legends and find real flesh-and-blood women who served their people in the name of Christian faith.

A STAFF TO THE PILGRIM

1

SAINT ITA

JANUARY 15

CHAPTER 1

Simplicity

ST ITA

A Saint who Understood Simplicity

Two woman saints stand tall in Irish tradition: Brigid, who is known by many, and Ita, who should be. Ita is a saint of Ireland who lived ca. 480-570. She is remembered as an organizer and spiritual director, but we turn to her for an emphasis upon simplicity in the lives of the Celtic saints.

Ita was born in County Waterford about 480 and named Deirdre at her baptism. Ita, the name she later received, comes from Gaelic for thirst. It was her obvious thirst for God's love that caused her to be given this name. Her father wanted her to marry, but she protested and eventually became a nun. In those days, a woman retained her independence and engaged in a career by monastic profession. Women monastics like Ita were (and are) talented and innovative people, who exhibit both organizing skills and spiritual insight and wisdom.

As an organizer, Ita established a community of nuns at Hy Conaill in County Limerick in southwest Ireland, which would later be called Killeedy, "the church of Ita." Since monasteries were also centers of art and education, Ita organized a boys' school at Killeedy.

As a boy, St Brendan the Navigator was one of Ita's pupils. He once asked her what three things God loved most. Ita famously answered that we should seek faith with a pure heart, simplicity of life, and generosity out of love. Furthermore, we should shun their opposites: hatred of others, resentment borne in the heart, and greed or excessive concern about wealth.

St Ita's legendary devotion focused on the Blessed Holy Trinity. Her single-minded devotion attracted many women to her monastery. A great deal of people came to Ita for spiritual guidance and wise counsel, and she became a "soul friend" to many. God granted her spiritual discernment and organizing skill in equal parts.

It was the simplicity of her heart that allowed her to focus upon others in such a way as to listen to them, to really hear them, and to bring them thus into not only confession of sin but also renewal of life. This is part of the gift of simplicity; it allows us to eschew distractions in the service of others.

According to one legend, Ita struggled with the devil for three days and three nights during a period of fasting. It was clear that the devil was losing, and in the end he confessed, "Ita, you will free yourself from me, and many others too will be delivered." Ita's focus on the love of God and the simplicity of life no doubt enabled her to overcome the temptations that would have brought others down.

Ita died around 570 at the age of ninety. Alcuin (eighth century), who organized education for Charlemagne, called her "foster mother of all the saints of Ireland" in his poem about the Irish saints.

The ruins of her monastery remain to this day, and pilgrims often decorate her grave with flowers. Her day in the calendar of saints is January 15.

TROPAR

Casting aside thy royal rank,
And embracing the godly monastic life,
Thou didst found a renowned school of piety,
Wherein thou didst nurture the souls of saints in
    reverence and the knowledge of God;
And having thus labored to please thy Bridegroom
    and Master,
Thou hast moved all the land of Erin to cry
    unto Him:
Have pity on us, O Lord of all,
And grant that we may ever stand with Ita at Thy
    right hand!
Holy Mother Ita, pray to God for us.

Simplicity and the Spiritual Life

God is not the reward of our search for God. God is present in all of life, and it is our task to discover God. Spiritual disciplines can unblock the channels of communication and vision between us: communication, because we lose the ability to hear God in the din and roar of our own inner chatter and the words the world hurls at us, and vision, because we lose the ability to see God's Presence in a world where pain mingles with pleasure and suffering with joy.

Prayer, fasting, and other disciplines are means to experience God through our senses once again.

The spiritual life begins and ends in poverty. In some senses this is another word for simplicity as over against duplicity. Saints like Ita are models of simplicity; their lack of guile is astonishing. They show us that we stand impoverished before God, with no riches to offer to buy the presence of God. Our poverty is, on the other hand, the major asset we bring before God, insofar as we acknowledge and reflect on it. We cannot own the riches of God; they must come as gift. For us to be gifted, we must recognize how poor we are: "Blessed are the poor in spirit, for theirs is the kingdom of heaven."

We are poor in many ways:

- because we move toward *death*, and nothing can buy us life
- because we are *unique*, and nothing can buy us the life another person leads; we must learn to accept our own lives and ourselves as we are
- because we are *needy*, and nothing can buy us out of need for the natural, material, and human resources by which we live
- because we have *limits*, and nothing can expand those limits; we were born in a particular time of particular parents with a particular heritage and particular physical limitations which become more evident as we grow older
- because we are *vulnerable*, and to become more fully human we must increase our vulnerability by loving.

The spiritual life calls us to recognize and live with our poverty. It is only by accepting our poverty that we learn to live in history and stop imagining fantasy lives in which we "escape history."

Our poverty becomes an asset when it becomes simplicity. Simplicity does not mean simplemindedness. It means, first of all, the opposite of duplicity. Duplicity means that we operate with a host of different agenda items, rather than to realize and embrace what the Danish theologian Søren Kierkegaard offers: "Purity of heart is to will one thing."

We must avoid all multiplicity of motives as we approach God with but one motive that may be expressed in several ways: "What is the will of God for my life?" or "How may I give glory to God through my living?" or "How can I will just one thing?" Prayer centers on seeking the answers to these questions.

Simplicity may also mean freedom from artificiality. Saints like Ita exhibit the purity which we seek to manifest in our own lives, though we so often fall short.

Simplicity directs us to be attentive to the here-and-now, to cut off our frustrating worry or fretting about the future and our endless recitation of the past. Simplicity calls us to live "just as I am, without one plea." To this end we seek prayer.

Prayer begins and ends in silence. It begins with our silence in the presence of God and ends with our presence in the silence of God.

All prayer rests on the prior word of God which emerges out of the silence – God has "spoken" to the world in creation, in the act of love in Christ, and through the Spirit. Prayer is one response to that word, whether alone or in community. Through prayer our poverty and our simplicity are both affirmed and transformed, and the spiritual life is born.

Simply Standing on the Lasting Platform of Faith

Back in our college days, we talked late into the evenings. We explored the place of Jesus in our faith, the role of the church, how Jesus could be called divine. These were matters of life and death to us. One of our conversation partners was my friend James, now of blessed memory. Urbane, sophisticated, slightly aloof, James was one of the smartest men in our class. Late one night four of us debated fine points of theology as only seniors can do. Suddenly, James said, "I won't debate this any more. I'm willing to accept the basics and move on. Life is too short to endlessly argue what the church settled over a thousand years ago."

After James earned his Ph.D., he taught for a quarter century in another country, unable to obtain a position in the U.S. because he had been educated beyond the presuppositions of our church – as we all had been, in one way or another.

This much you must know: as students, we did not accept the church's faith without deep questioning, argument, and exploration. Our professors drove us to think, and think again, about matters of faith from many angles: psychological, philosophical, linguistic, scientific. They pushed us to the limit so that we could affirm the core faith in the midst of doubt, affirm tradition in the midst of novelty, and use our questions to move more deeply into that tradition. This was no easy task, and some students who could not accept the challenge or surmount the scholastic rigors fell by the wayside. Many of us eventually became unacceptable to the church of our youth, although – and here is the point – we did not give up the faith. We built upon the platform, just as my friend James had suggested so many years ago.

Fifty years after he said it, James' insight still remains quite acceptable to me. Life is too short to endlessly argue what the church settled over a thousand years ago. The platform for full-bodied, robust faith does not offer security; it offers a springboard for development.

This idea of a platform may be hard to comprehend; we are a quizzical and cynical society, and most people will not accept the church's platform as foundational. But the generations of teachers who went before us were not our intellectual inferiors. They did not ask for mindless, uncritical acceptance. They toiled intellectually for centuries to construct a platform that would withstand the passage of time and the erosion of simplistic faith.

I see and hear many people who want to construct their own personal platform of faith. But that means that they must start from square one every time they think about faith. Nothing is ever settled, nothing becomes a solid platform one can build on. Since everything is based on starting over, they make faith up as they go along, or so it seems. And they can never advance beyond square one. I speak against this restless and endless reliance upon the inventions of our own minds. There is solid rock beneath us if we take the time to work with it.

What is the platform? Some call it the Creed. It is a summary of faith that rests upon the witness of the Bible, especially the New Testament, to the faith received from Israel and in and through Jesus of Nazareth, "true God and true man." Yes it is historically conditioned. Yes, it requires interpretation. But it remains the platform from which the faith can expand into all of life rather than implode upon itself.

We do not have to start over again every time. We have inherited a core that is simple but not simplistic. The saints knew this, and St Ita professed it in her monastery and to her pupils. The rock stands.

The Unity and Simplicity of Organized Religion

Occasionally I have to remind people who say, "I don't believe in organized religion," that, although there may be religion without organization, every form of spiritual development and exploration worth its salt in the history of the world eventually became organized. And with good reason.

Throughout history, people clustered around recipients of revelations or inaugurators of spiritual movements because they saw in them truth that they could not ferret out for themselves. Whether or not the followers were able to attain unto the spiritual heights of the leaders is a different story; on occasion these mimickers ended up making degenerate attempts to force people to accept their truths. We see this in history. "Oh no," as Monty Python would say, "Not the Spanish Inquisition!" But that is not the whole story.

There were also those who mined the resources they were given and in fact drove the insights they received much deeper. Would this not be a worthy project? This is what we see with movements like the Desert Fathers and Mothers in early Christianity. These people took the initial impetus of their founder's faith and discovered or invented ways to enable ordinary people to attain spiritual wholeness. In other words, they created pathways to follow. They did this in an organized fashion, systematizing without creating a "system," organizing without creating an institution. This, too, occurred across history, and it seems to me a good thing.

It is my opinion, of course, but I think people dislike "organized religion" because there are dues to be paid, and not many people are willing to pay them. When I say that, I am not thinking of money. I am thinking of the spiritual struggles we endure in order to take the pathway that leads to the burning center of our faith. I am thinking of the fact that we have to achieve a baseline of morality before we can advance to the height of spirituality. We have to agree that the universe requires certain behaviors: not stealing, not bearing false witness, not committing murder, not engaging in idolatry or adultery (they are related), and so forth. Only when we start with these disciplines can we proceed on the path. But many people balk at these markers on the way, and thus bail out on "organized religion," as they call it.

I grant that Jesus never thought he would become the CEO of a large corporation, but he was not without a pathway. As a faithful Jew he knew that the path led from the commandments to a deeper reality. We have inherited this awareness and action.

In our Orthodox Christian tradition, a simple one-way highway, having two lanes, leads into the heart of the faith. The two lanes, namely the sacramental life and the ascetic disciplines, proceed together. They lead into life with God through different, but complementary, ways of participation. The ascetic lane is paved by prayer, fasting, charity, and observance of the commandments. The sacramental lane is paved by baptism, anointing in the Spirit, participation in the Lord's Supper, and confession. The lanes belong together, and we have no other road. These are not gimmicks or techniques; they are the way of faith. We have no spectacular methods beyond this. There is no esoteric spirituality, no magic sign, and no secret word. All we can offer is this hard uphill pathway. St Ita (and other monastic leaders like her) recognized and taught this basic truth to her students. The results are manifest in those who, like St Brendan, followed in her footsteps.

You may not want "organized religion." But if you are looking for a spiritual pathway, it must have markers, guidelines, and clear guidance.

That is what the ascetic path is all about. The path is worth embracing, and it can only be followed through some form of organization.

From Simplicity to Complexity and Back: Reaching Across the Borderlines of Religion

"In the beginning," we are told, what we today call art and myth and dance and ritual were all one. The academic branch known as ritual studies tells us that long ago people danced their stories, narrated their hopes, and inscribed their insights onto walls. They made rituals that told who they were, where they came from, and what they wanted life to be like.

If both archaeology and anthropology, and to some extent, history, all support this view, how did we arrive at the point where all this richly-textured complexity became compartmentalized? How was the notion of religion coined? How was such a broad concept as "religion" reduced to a set of beliefs? And most tragically, how did we get to the point where people pick up an Uzi or a Kalashnikov and gun down others who hold a different grab bag of beliefs?

There is, of course, no direct line from point A to point Z, from original unity to total separation. Everything is jagged, uneven, and spotty. But it is clear that this process of separation eventually led to unfortunate consequences.

Jewish scholar Daniel Boyarin thinks it began, at least in one area, with the separation that occurred during and after the formative periods in Judaism and Christianity. Christianity was originally a Jewish movement, but over the course of time it became primarily composed of people who were not Jews. That much most people know – or think we know.

In his masterful book *Border Lines*, Boyarin erases the neatness of this distinction. He shows that in the earliest period, distinctions between Jew and Christian were fluid and mobile. The lines were blurred; people were not strictly separated into Jews and non-Jews. Rather, everyone lived on a broad cultural map that offered many choices for belief and behavior.

Over the first four centuries of the Common Era, various thinkers began to set up standards that divided people into two camps, Jews and non-Jews. Non-Jews were now mostly Christian. Christians led this divisive movement, but Jews also contributed to the separation. These separatist movements were not yet identified as religions because "religion" did not yet exist as a fixed set of beliefs or behaviors applied in advance to movements. That required one more step.

For that step to be taken, "border makers" arose who constructed a fixed and separate identity for both Judaism and Christianity. These border makers wrote the laundry lists that came to define the meaning of "Christian" and "Jew" and created religion as a category.

The final step connected political clout to "religion." That step enforced the distinctions, and thus gave Christians clear economic and political advantage over Jews. This happened in the fifth and sixth centuries, after which Jews were systematically disenfranchised throughout rising and falling empires, up through the Holocaust.

We cannot turn back the hands of time, but much blood and heartache could have been avoided had people stayed on the broad cultural map and not created these borderlines.

If we could accept that, "in the beginning," art and myth and dance and ritual were unified, we could reach across divisions to embrace one another as seekers after the one truth that is manifest among us in many different ways. Our lives would be enriched rather than diminished or threatened.

It is possible to hold one's set of beliefs and behaviors as truth – I certainly do – without rejecting others'. We must be open to dialogue, but that does not require us to accept others' ideas and beliefs uncritically. We have to find a non-violent way to engage in correlation – in the comparison of one another's beliefs to find connections and underlying threads. That way leads to peace while respecting differences.

The Simplicity of Our Daily Bread - My Visit with M. Poilâne

The year 1989 marked the 200th anniversary of the French Revolution. To celebrate the occasion, Marshall Field's – the grand old Chicago department store – sponsored a series of lectures and workshops with renowned French chefs.

Lionel Poilâne, a famous French *boulanger* (bread baker), was one of the six cooks who came to Chicago. At age fifteen, when he was working for his father (a successful Paris *boulanger*), young Poilâne had cycled the French countryside in search of authentic old and rustic recipes. Lionel went on to become famous throughout France and worldwide for his country whole wheat loaves, which are still flown into big cities like Chicago and New York daily.

Poilâne's exploration of the history of French baking and breads resuscitated his industry and inspired bakers to return to earlier kinds of whole grain and natural leaven breads, to the *pain de campagne* of older days. Some would credit Poilâne with originating the new artisan bread movement. He was able to open up baking as a way of life.

As a committed baker, I virtually ran to Poilâne's lecture on that cold March day. As he spoke, I knew this was a man completely full of his work in the very best sense. Intense, animated, and vibrant, he spoke with deep passion and ardent love about his work. I was enchanted as I became aware that bread was at the heart of his spiritual vision, just as it is for me.

Bread was also central to Jesus' spiritual vision. In good Jewish fashion, he spent much time at festive dinner tables with his disciples, and his vision of God's reign is that of a great banquet or a wedding feast. I want only to be one of the bakers there.

When the lecture was over, we ate M. Poilâne's different breads with cheese and wine. When he sat down close to me, I made bold to ask him about his spiritual vision of bread. He seemed genuinely pleased that someone had seen this vision, and spoke about it eagerly. He told me that he saw a logical and clear connection between Holy Communion and baking, which seemed rather natural since he was of Catholic heritage. He saw his baking as a sort of extension of the sacrament – with himself as priest of the creation, if not of the church.

I learned several things that day. First, *you can transform necessity into pleasure.* We need our daily bread, but it should not be a burden. We can derive a great deal of pleasure from the taste, the smell, the texture, and the material of our daily bread. Since daily bread is a necessity, we might as well involve ourselves in the process and embrace the necessity as a craft, and by so doing transform the experience from need to pleasure. Here is a lesson for all of life.

The opposite is unfortunately also true: you can transform pleasure into necessity. The repetitive nature of many life tasks robs them of the pleasure they would give us if only we could approach them afresh each time.

Second, when all things are well with our hearts, it will be clear that *the spiritual and the sensual belong together.* They are married so that ordinary life bears extraordinary grace. The simplest things may, in fact, be most profound when you see them through eyes that wonder. "Give us this day our daily bread" reminds us to attend to the extraordinary nature of daily life. How simple this truth is, and yet how profound.

Returning our thoughts to St Ita, I am convinced that the Celtic monastic tradition which she embodied was able to see depth in the midst of surface, simplicity in the midst of complexity, and the divine in the midst of the human. This vision of simplicity breathed lifeblood into the Celtic tradition, and can do so again for us in our age.

Mending

My mother darned socks. She had a black darning bob over which she placed my socks to mend the hole. Even when there was more money, she still darned socks – and replaced buttons, sewed hems, patched trousers, and turned collars around to make shirts last longer. She prized the value in mending. My father was rather hapless as a mechanic, but he also did his best to fix things because he valued living that way. Fixing things was a value I grew up with, along with all sorts of "recycling" we did before the word was invented.

Contrast this with today's throwaway world. A number of years ago, I went to the trouble of dismantling our car radio and taking it to an automobile radio shop to have it fixed. The electrician looked at me as if I was crazy. "Nobody fixes these things anymore. You just replace them and throw the old ones away." Yes, I know we have made great strides in recycling, but there is still so much waste.

Is there a connection between a throwaway culture and throwaway people? Maybe. Could it be that the more trash there is on the highway, the more blasé we become about the attitude that people might be trash, too? I hope not. But who knows? The connection is worth pondering.

Spirituality has something to teach us on the subject of mending vs. discarding. Spirituality is not woozy or wooly-minded. Rather, it is practical. It begins with not letting our egos stand between us and the small calls to service we can all answer. If something is broken, fix it. Do not think about it. If there is trash on the ground, pick it up. Do not let ego interfere. If someone is in need, reach out to him or her. Let us push ourselves out of the way to be present to another human being, without pandering and without patronization. This is simplicity at its core: doing what is right in front of us without thinking about it.

The beloved Roman Catholic writer Henri Nouwen said that we are all wounded healers. When Jacob wrestled with the angel, and said he would not let go without a blessing, the angel's blessing came with a wrenching that made him limp for the rest of his life. Now I am limping through this world, and so are you. But together we can heal one another; together we can be blessings one to another.

Do not worry if you are yourself in need. We all are. We are all broken. A long time ago a Jewish adherent to Jesus named Saul/Paul wrote that God's graceful presence in our lives is only displayed through "broken vessels." We are cracked pots, so to speak, and whatever Light of God we have to shed only comes through our brokenness.

The Jewish mystical tradition of Kabbalah picks up this imagery and turns it once more. According to Rabbi Isaac Luria, founder of the movement, God intended to create the world with vessels of Light, but the Light was too strong. So everything shattered into little bits, like glass on the pavement after a car accident. Now we must assist God, first, by resolving not to add to the brokenness by violence and hatred; and second, by mending the vessels that were supposed to bear Light into the world.

These images remind us that we are not finished, nor is our world. We are constantly engaged in living. We are never able to stop with "life." In fact, to stop with life as if it were a finished project is to cross the threshold to death. But that is another matter.

Meanwhile, let us seek to repair the world (Hebrew, *tikkun ha-olam*), one sock at a time.

The Exquisite Beauty of the Simple Gifts

The old Shaker hymn says, "'Tis a gift to be simple, 'tis a gift to be free; 'tis a gift to come down where you ought to be." As you look at Shaker furniture, architecture, or woven crafts, you see the truth of that hymn wrought in material objects. And you see the beauty. In my living room sits a stool that, although not Shaker, was built by a true craftsman, a friend of mine from long ago. Its beauty is in its simplicity, and its simplicity is its truth.

The simple gifts in life come to us through the common senses we share: taste and touch, hearing and seeing, smell and movement. Those people who are deprived of one sense are frequently gifted with more intensity in the others to compensate for their loss.

The great British stone-carver and calligrapher Eric Gill said, "Look after truth and goodness, and beauty will look after herself." He meant that beauty proceeds from simplicity, from clean design, and from the marriage of design and purpose. That sort of beauty is, in fact, goodness. For Gill, art and craft blended and could neither be discerned nor discussed separately. I tend to follow Gill and his disciples in my own crafts. Gill affirmed that a well-wrought carved wooden spoon could be displayed next to a Rembrandt painting. To Eric Gill, my friend's stool would not be out of place in a museum – except that to place it there would take it out of its proper place, and rob it of its purpose.

So often people look for spiritual value in places beyond the ordinary. Look at all the spiritual gurus in America who have come and gone over the last forty years, and you will see what I mean. Many of these folks promised spiritual depth, but at a price: giving up your independence to their thinking, your behavior to their actions, and of course your money to their pockets. The siren call of exotic and esoteric spirituality continues to be heard across the land, although perhaps not as loudly as in a previous generation. It beckons those who do not realize the sacredness of the ordinary.

Old railroad crossing signs used to simply say, "Stop, look, and listen." We can use this as a motto for our lives. Open the kitchen drawer and look at the incredible marriage of design and purpose in a hand-cranked eggbeater. Open the door and listen to the repertoire of the western Mockingbird. Sit on that wooden stool and feel its integrity. Feel the wind on your face as you walk briskly through your neighborhood. Here is where spiritual stuff can be found; we do not need to go outside the bounds of everyday life.

Some forms of Christianity discouraged appreciation of these simple experiences as if they were pagan, and thus to be shunned or avoided. But if we do not believe that God, however envisioned, addresses us through the ordinary stuff of life, then we have betrayed the core message of Christianity and, for that matter, of all religious experience.

In everyday life we bake bread, make a home, walk in the park, talk with friends and fellow workers about small stuff. It is all ordinary, but it is our life, so why not enjoy it? In fact, ordinary life is ours to enjoy.

We may not notice the ordinary. Catholic theologian Karl Rahner wrote that we live in grace as fish do in water. Does a fish notice the water in which it swims? Only if it jumps out of the pool. We find it hard to remember ordinary blessings. Our traditions teach us to beware the extraordinary, since we put too much stock in it and forget ordinary blessings all the more. We tend to idolize the extraordinary, but we live in the ordinary.

Monumental tragedy is also an extraordinary experience, and it brings a sense of God's presence known in absence, as in, "where was God when…?" The tragedy may be so staggering in weight and complexity that we remember the holiness of the ordinary in stark contrast to the horrifying evil. We do not wake up in the morning and think that perhaps today someone will fly an airplane into my workplace and kill me and thousands of other people in a wanton act of destruction. That is not ordinary. We all sit up in bed, yawn, scratch our spouse's back if we are privileged to have one, get up, get dressed, and do our daily routine.

We count on life to be ordinary. Ordinariness makes life manageable, which makes it all the more incredible to turn on our TV and discover that our world has been blown apart, that a familiar skyline is being rearranged by destruction rather than by construction. 9/11, as it is now universally known, was extraordinary. Twenty people killed by suicide bombers in Pakistan or Iraq – that is also extraordinary. When these events become ordinary, we have become callous and callow, numbed into submission to evil.

St Ita, patron saint of both simplicity and blessing, taught us to thank God for the grace of the ordinary. To thank God for the presence of those who enhance the ordinariness of our lives. To thank God for the small issues we deal with from day to day, from crabgrass to crabby relatives, from school deadlines and candy sales to job hassles. Let us not make idols of the extraordinary, because when we do, we lose sight of the One who is seen veiled through the ordinary. Let us not forget to bless the ordinary gifts and people who grace our lives.

Keep in prayer those who have lost their lives or their loves through extraordinary acts of violence. These are not normal things. They are the face of evil in our time. But do not let them obscure the face of God, who may be known best in and through the ordinary – even when we sometimes fail to notice.

2

SAINT CUTHBERT

MARCH 20

CHAPTER 2

Silence

ST CUTHBERT

The Venerable Bede recorded the life of St Cuthbert. He swore to its accuracy and authenticity because he was quite fond of Cuthbert and wanted to make sure his readers knew Cuthbert was a genuine saint of the people. Although he came to be considered a "Celtic" saint because of his spiritual training and life, Cuthbert was born an Anglo-Saxon, which is another reason why Bede revered him. In his *History*, Bede exhibited a not-so-subtle preference for the Anglo-Saxon leaders of the early British church.

Cuthbert (634-687) had a vision of a shaft of light descending to earth from heaven while he was serving with a shepherd in the Lammermuir Hills in southern Scotland. He interpreted this vision of a holy person being borne to heaven from earth as a sign that he was to become a monk, and that he should therefore follow the footsteps of Aidan to Holy Island – Lindisfarne – off the northeast coast of England near the Scottish border.

Cuthbert began his monastic life at Melrose Abbey where the Irish monk Boisil was abbot. Thus, like many Anglo-Saxon Christians, he received his education at the hands of Celtic teachers. From Melrose he progressed to Ripon, where he served as guest master. After some difficulties he returned to Melrose and became abbot after the repose of Boisil.

The newly-appointed abbot of Lindisfarne, Eata, who had been prior at Ripon, requested that Cuthbert go with him to Holy Island. By this time Cuthbert had a reputation as a hermit monk who spent much time in silence and travel to surrounding areas, meeting people and inviting them into the faith. He made a hermitage on Lindisfarne but also had a refuge on Inner Farne, which to this day remains a place of pilgrimage.

Cuthbert was caught up in the strife between the Roman and Celtic factions of the church that came to a head in the so-called Synod of Whitby (664), presided over by the abbess Hilda of Whitby (see chapter five). Despite his Anglo-Saxon background, Cuthbert wanted to find common ground and harmony between the factions. When the Synod, in his eyes, capitulated to Roman demands, he sought even deeper refuge in silence and retreat at his hermitage on Inner Farne, relinquishing his post as prior of Lindisfarne. He lived there for almost a decade, sought out as a spiritual father by many who knew his reputation as a saintly and silent leader. Eventually he was brought back to serve the larger church, this time as Bishop of Lindisfarne, a post that covered the entire area of Northumberland.

As bishop, Cuthbert retained his concern for animals and the poor, and he was greatly loved by the people in his diocese. Unlike many authoritarian rulers of both church and state, he sought counsel and decision by consensus. In his own words: "Preserve divine charity among yourself, and when you come together to discuss your common affairs let your principal goal be to reach unanimous decision." His rule of silence gave him deep awareness of the condition of humanity, as silence can do for those who use it as a tool for insight and contemplation of their own condition.

Over a century after Cuthbert's death, with Vikings breathing off the shores of Holy Island, the monks exhumed his body and carried him off. In 793 they settled on an inland spot indicated by the sign of a dun cow. There they erected a church in which he was buried. Cuthbert remains entombed in this church, now Durham Cathedral, to this day. We celebrate St Cuthbert on March 20.

TROPAR

> While still in your youth, you laid aside all
>   worldly cares,
> And took up the sweet yoke of Christ,
> And you were shown forth in truth to be nobly
>   radiant in the grace of the Holy Spirit.
> Therefore, God established you as a rule of faith
>   and shepherd of His radiant flock,
> Godly-minded Cuthbert,
> Converser with angels and intercessor for men.

Make Every Word a Sacrifice

These days we are surrounded by noise everywhere we go, especially if we keep the car radio on while we drive. We can hardly escape words, most of them cheap; many of them empty. They are simply fillers, like the lines that used to be at the bottom of newspaper columns when they did not have enough news to fill the whole column: "The potato production of the country of Azerbaijan was four million pounds last year. . . ."

We get into trouble when we forget that words are supposed to count, that empty words are useless. We go down pathways of gossip or complaints. When I overhear people talk in public, it seems like ninety percent of what I hear falls into one of those two categories. Perhaps, as they say, a lot of speech is simply to enable people to make connections. But I am unsure about the need to talk about or against others that seems to occupy so many people I overhear.

This reminds me of sayings from the ancient monks known as the Fathers and Mothers of the Desert. These folks went out from cities like Alexandria and Antioch into the desert, mostly to find peace and quiet, because they knew instinctively that the noise and jabber of the cities was a huge distraction. They reasoned that, if they wanted to experience God, they had to get rid of the distractions. Abba Moses the Ethiopian, a formidable physical presence, said it well: "It is impossible to have Christ continually in your heart without silence, humility, and unceasing prayer," and he knew that the second two qualities were, in large part, a result of the first.

The Bishop of Alexandria, one Theophilus, came out to the desert to visit. Monks urged Abba Pambo, one of the best known of the Desert Fathers, to prepare some words to "edify his soul in this place." Whereupon Pambo replied, "If he is not edified by my silence, there is no hope that he will be edified by my words." This may be hard for some people to understand, particularly those who think that the only way we establish contact and rapport with others is through our speaking. But Pambo had a point; his life was his major speech. So it should be with us.

I was deeply impressed by a small book that came out during the latter days of the Communist regime in Russia. It is entitled *Talking About God is Dangerous*, by Tatiana Goricheva. She was a member of one of the many underground movements that were quietly reviving Christian faith in that bruised and tormented land. Goricheva's journey from atheist intellectual to intelligent Christian is itself worthy of consideration. But the sentence on page 91 of her book that burned into me is this: "Every word must be a sacrifice – filled to the brim with authenticity. Otherwise it is better to keep silent."

I believe this, even though sometimes I get caught up in the circuit of speech that leads to a surfeit of words. We know when we are not authentic, when our own words ring hollow and we are just filling space with noise. Then it is best to back off, assess the situation, discover why we feel the need to prattle on, and recede into silence. In silence we will find the authenticity that is so important to communicate, if words are to bear true meaning for us and for others.

It is No Longer Quiet Out Here

My mother, who was born in the late 1800s, lived to be

just shy of 96. When she was quite old we asked her to write a memoir for a family newsletter. Although she was reluctant, claiming nothing of interest in her life, I insisted. I was proud of her for many reasons, one being that she was among the relatively small number of women who graduated from high school in the early years of the 20th century. She finally wrote a short memoir. It began:

> "When I was a child it was quiet. There was no radio. There were very few automobiles and no airplanes. If we heard a car we would run out into the street to see it go past, because it was so unusual. There was a lot of silence."

"When I was a child it was quiet." Nobody is ever going to say that again. We are surrounded by radio, television, computers, and phones, constantly tuned in to the world around us, or so we think. Planes and cars and motorcycles are everywhere. We cannot escape noise anywhere. There are no more secluded mountain retreats.

Of course we are not talking about noise indiscriminately. The woods are full of noise, as anyone who has spent time in them knows. So are farms and ranches. It is the quality of the noise that is different, the natural versus the unnatural.

People walk around plugged into noise, even if it is called music, or talk radio, or NPR. I fly often, and I notice that I am typically the only person reading an actual book or just sitting quietly. Everyone around me is listening to a recording device or plugged into a computer. On the road, I see drivers with headphones – maybe they are trying to substitute one noise for another. People are not only beset by noise around them; many actually choose to increase the noise. We cannot even enter a grocery store anymore without being greeted with piped-in music.

"So what," you say; "It's just the way life has gone in this 21st century."

But let me suggest that there is a price to pay. The Psalmist says, "Be silent and know that I am God." When we are surrounded by noise, we cannot hear ourselves think. And there is the problem. So many people, I am convinced, fill their lives with noise because they cannot afford to be quiet or silent. In silence, they will have to confront the emptiness that is inside them.

My mother was a woman of deep faith. Even in her worst moments, and there were many over her long years, she was unafraid to confront the silence and the quiet because she knew the Presence of God in them. In fact, to the end of her life she cherished quiet moments, times of meditation and prayer.

When we fill our lives with noise, the emptiness inside us increases, rather than decreases. We lose the inner link to our source of life, whom we name God. Without quiet outside, the chances are slim that we will find the genuine quiet inside in which God is known. "My soul for God in silence waits." The Psalmist assumes that our inner self is fulfilled through the medium of silence, and that the Living God will address us there. In waiting for God, we wait quietly. Like my mother. Like the contemplatives of all traditions. Let us return to the silence.

Silence and Overcoming Distractions

Lama Govinda, the great Tibetan Buddhist master, wrote that there is a "spiritual force that requires no philosophical argument or intellectual justification, because it is not based on theoretical knowledge but on...direct experience." The Zen Buddhist might say that we can attain direct perception into the heart of reality. We might say, "Be still and know that I am God."

Deep spiritual realities are best entered by experience rather than by thought. These realities may be ultimately incommunicable because no amount of words can adequately describe the inner meeting of the soul with God – though we must try in order to share. Paradoxically, the act of thinking about such meetings automatically removes us from the experience. It is funny how that works. If I catch the butterfly I can no longer experience the butterfly in flight. No wonder Chicago theologian Langdon Gilkey spoke of God's "fragile presence."

Feminist theologian Nelle Morton used the image of God as the Listener who, listening to our deepest cries and whispers, can hear us into speech. God will not overwhelm us with loudness and fanfare, but may be known instead as the "voice of silence" that came to Elijah in his cave (I Kings 19:12), like a gentle breeze, so slight that we can hardly feel it, soft as a feather on the cheek.

If we wish to feel the breeze or hear the whisper, to not crush the fragile Presence, to watch the butterfly, we must be quiet and pay attention. Attentiveness is the first order, and in our society it is difficult to achieve.

Attentiveness is difficult to achieve because we are distracted to the "nth degree." Our ability to live in quiet is overwhelmed by the toys of our culture: radio, TV, movies, computers, cell phones, music players. We jokingly remember the days when Timothy Leary urged us to "turn on, tune in, and drop out." He had LSD in mind; he would be chuckling to see how we have interpreted his words in this day of electronic gizmos. It is as if we do not know we exist unless we are hearing or seeing something that demands our attention and takes us out of the experience of the present moment. We only know we are here because we are excited or titillated. As the social critic Neil Postman said in the title of one of his best books, we are "amusing ourselves to death."

Losing distractions and gaining quiet are not in themselves the goal. But whatever goal is met by attaining quiet and solitude, it surely will not come until we find that inner silence that is offered when we put ourselves in a position to discover it. And that position requires outer quiet as well. Quiet is the threshold, not the doorway, but there can be no door without the threshold.

Our distractions – which are also deceptions – lead to callousness and a false idea of normalcy. Rabbi Abraham Joshua Heschel defined sin as callousness. We become calloused against God's presence because we are callous to the pain of our world and, in fact, to our own lostness. We accept as normalcy that people are insensitive, defensive, rude, and aloof from others. Our distractions make us think and act this way, causing us to put so much energy into sustaining them that we become insensitive and blind. Under such circumstances the Presence can be terrifying. But when we turn from our callousness, take off the blinders, and open ourselves at a deep level, the Presence brings healing and light.

We have to cross the threshold and wait expectantly for the Presence to enfold us. Even if we do not yet know how to name it, that Presence will come. Be still.

Finding a Place for Awe

We like to think of ourselves as rational creatures. That is what separates us from the animals, right? Well, think again. With the slightest provocation, we abandon our reasonable heads and jump into acts driven by emotion or, more precisely, passion. Extraordinary emotional responses can overwhelm our sensibility and common sense in any moment and drag us to a place where we normally do not want to be.

What does this have to do with finding awe in our lives again? A lot. The mystics of the church, and in other religions as well, speak to us of the need to first become ethical persons. Then, and only then, are we prepared to walk further on the spiritual path. We have a propensity to stumble and fall into easy trespassing. That is why it is crucial to achieve grounding beyond the passions. Only when this occurs are we fit for the spiritual path. That is the testimony of the elders, and we do well to hear and observe it.

Since the path to awe travels through ethics, our morality and our mysticism are not separate aspects of our lives. They begin and belong together. Nor are nature and the human divided. We are a part of, not apart from, the natural world. We humans have to honor nature in an ethical way to achieve awe in the presence of the natural world. It will not do to exploit, abuse, manipulate, exhaust, or otherwise misuse the natural world, not if we want to stand before nature in awe. Wonder emerges from respect and appreciation, from observing ecosystems and how they work marvelously well if we leave them alone.

The same thing is true of human beings. We stand in awe before others when we view them as wholes, not as parts or even as the sum of parts. Lust makes us concentrate on parts; love lets us appreciate the whole person. So let there be no abuse, no exploitation here, neither here nor in the natural realm.

When we embrace our world properly, we stop clinging to it for improper reasons such as lust, pride, envy, and greed. Any one of the seven deadly sins can be the basis for the sort of clinging I have in mind. But when we move past the clinging, cloying side of the passions and discover the "there-ness" of what or who is there, we emerge into new light. In our circles, we could say that we have learned to cleave our souls to God. This cleaving frees us from clinging to things that are not ultimate. This is a tough concept to apprehend; so often we want to grasp and grab things that are not ultimate, which are decaying and dying all around us, or which offer us but momentary satisfaction. St Augustine said, "Our hearts are restless until they find their rest in Thee." The restlessness is there because we cling to that which is not ultimate, eternal, and infinite. In short, we "fall short of the glory of God."

The good news is that, once we find our rest in the ultimate, we are free to embrace, appreciate, and savor what is not ultimate – but without being hooked by it. We are freed for awe, and we enter the palace of wonder once again. Wonder is the first step in discovering how to live in an awesome place, but we can only get to it through treading the ethical pathway. This sounds very flat-footed and somewhat hard, and indeed it is. But it is the right way to proceed. Awe arises out of respect, and respect is displayed by acting ethically.

Silence and Finding Our Authentic Voice

When he was seven years old, our grandson gave us the gift of an important insight. When his mother asked him what was the most important part of his body, he pointed to his heart. She asked him why that was most important. He said, "That's where your voice comes from, and your soul speaks through your voice."

We have all known people who came across as inauthentic. Most often we discover this by listening carefully to the shape of their voice. Something is absent. We cannot detect any soul in it. Not only disembodied, that voice is also empty of soul, and thus empty of heart.

Perhaps we, ourselves, have been one of those who seem inauthentic. It is not easy to come into the fullness of voice, to emerge from silence into truthfulness and candor when we converse with others.

When I was a professor in Chicago, I taught a course entitled *Silence and Speech*. Its basic premise was that true silence is essential for truthfulness in speech and, conversely, true speaking reveals our inner silences. I think our grandson has figured this out at an early age, and I hope the knocks of life do not dislodge his insight.

The novelist and essayist Pico Iyer wrote, "We have to earn silence, to work for it: to make it not an absence but a presence;

not emptiness but repletion. …We all know how treacherous are words, and how often we use them to paper over embarrassment, or emptiness, or fear of the larger spaces that silence brings. 'Words, words, words' commit us to positions we do not really hold, the imperatives of chatter; words are what we use for lies, false promises and gossip" (TIME essay, January 25, 1993). Iyer is onto truth here, but I think it incomplete. What I miss is the note that genuine speech emerges out of true silence even as true silence issues forth in authentic speaking. Thus are the lies avoided, thus do we become truly present, and thus does the soul speak.

The world is full of babble. It surrounds us on all sides, seeps into our lives via radio, television, and all of the other devices that invade our space and rob our silence. Words have become cheaper than ever before, it seems, and hence we distrust the voice.

Of course there are times when we do not know how to speak, and our silence is then a good thing. Confronted by death, confronted by love, confronted by suffering, speech falls away and we know the silence of empathy, the quiet of compassion. This silence is both logical and understandable. It requires a huge effort to speak anything of merit into the silence of suffering brought about by war and violence. The writer Alice Borchard Greene long ago said, "When the cargo of feeling is too heavy it sinks the frail craft of verbal response." Better to keep silent. Better to retreat to your heart where your voice comes from.

For many people in our society, the retreat to silence means only absence and not possibility, only void and not creative center. We have been so long drawn off silence by the noise that surrounds us that we think we are hollow when noise and words are absent. But it is not so.

We still have time to find that heart where the voice originates, where the soul can be expressed through the voice. Every spiritual tradition presents a way into silence through contemplation, meditation, or prayer. Find it in yours or find someone to help you enter it. The world is in need of authentic speech.

3

SAINT MELANGELL

MAY 27

CHAPTER 3

Solitude

ST MELANGELL

Sometimes people have to flee for their lives to find solitude. This flight may lead them to desolate and remote places. Such was the solitude St Melangell needed; such was the solitude she found in a new country across a sea.

St Melangell is the matron saint of God's creatures, and especially of rabbits. Her name is Melangell in Welsh (approximate English pronunciation: meh-*long*-gesh), but she is also known in the Latin *Life* written about her as *Monacella*, which means "little nun." She is one of only two Welsh women saints graced with a Latin *Life*, the other one being Gwenfrewi (whom see in chapter four).

We know not exactly which year in the sixth century Melangell was born, but the legend is that she was of royal birth in Ireland. As often happened back then, her father had chosen to give her in marriage to another royal; such marriages were arranged for convenience in achieving treaties across family lines. Although Melangell refused, her father pursued the matter. Faced with no alternative, she fled across the Irish Sea around 590 and took refuge in the remote Berwyn foothills area of North Wales simply called Pennant, where she lived as a solitary monastic before being "discovered." Melangell had a favorite slab rock upon which she preferred to sleep and, at first, she lived in a cave.

The discovery happened in this way: in the year 604, a hunter named Brochfael Ysgithrog, Prince of Powys (one of the six Cantrefs of Wales), was chasing hares with his hounds. He entered a wood and there saw a young woman sitting on the ground with her cloak gathered up around her; a hare was in the folds of the cloak peeping out with a frightened gaze upon the hounds who were set to attack. Instead of attacking, however, the hounds ran off in fright themselves. Her sanctity was so strong as to provide protection for the hare.

Prince Brochfael had never seen anyone like her before, nor had he experienced the rebuff of his hounds. He asked the woman her name. She replied that she was Melangell, and that she was absorbed in prayer when the hare ran to her for protection. The prince, duly impressed with both her beauty and her sanctity, gave her the lands surrounding the town as a sanctuary for both animals and people, and as a setting for her to establish a monastery.

St Melangell lived as a nun on that territory for another thirty-seven years, during which she gathered a small community of nuns who were committed to prayer and solitude. She established the area as a sanctuary and no hares, indeed, no animals at all were killed on those grounds. St Melangell died in 641.

The church at Pennant Melangell, built to honor the saint and containing her shrine, is tucked away in the remote Berwyn foothills of North Wales. It is reputedly the oldest Romanesque shrine in Britain, dating from the 12th century.

Pennant Melangell remains a quiet and remote place, with little to disturb one's solitude. It is easy to see why, surrounded by such natural beauty, Melangell desired to remain there for a life in prayer and counseling, offering sanctuary to those who sought her out, and to the animal life of the area. Today St Melangell is considered the premier Celtic saint of the environment. As we might expect, the icon of Melangell depicts her holding a hare. Her feast day is May 27.

TROPAR

> *Preferring the rigors of monasticism to worldly*
> *status and marriage,*
> *O pious Melangell,*
> *Thou wast fifteen years on a rock,*
> *Emulating the example of the Syrian Stylites.*
> *Wherefore, O Saint,*
> *Pray to God that He will give us strength to serve*
> *Him as He wills,*
> *That we may be found worthy of His great mercy.*

Letting Go as Spiritual Discipline

My mother lived to be almost 96. She was in fairly good shape until the last four years of her life, when a minor stroke rendered her unaware of her surroundings. When that happened, we had to close her apartment because she could no longer live alone.

Mother had outlived my father by thirty-five years, most of which she occupied the same second-floor walk-up apartment in Philadelphia. When the time came to empty her flat, we distributed her possessions among us and gave the key back to the landlord, an old family friend.

Three weeks later, Mother returned to full consciousness only to find that she was in a care facility for the aging. I was with her when she awoke. The conversation was simple.

"Is this where I live now?"

"Yes, Mother, it is. We had to close up the apartment because you won't be able to live on your own anymore."

After a short pause, she said, "The food's not bad."

So there it was. Thirty-five years in the same place given up in a flash. Most of her possessions were in storage in our several garages. The last of her friends was at a significant distance. And all she had to say was, "The food's not bad"?

When one of Mother's best friends was widowed, she told her daughter (also my friend) that she would move to California to live with her. My friend told her mother that she was welcome to do so, but wondered how long it would take her to arrange matters and clear out the house. In a surprisingly short time, she arrived at my friend's home with nothing but a clutch of suitcases. What had happened to the rest of the household goods from a house they had occupied for fifty years, she wondered. "Gave it all away," said her mom, and stepped over the threshold to a new life.

The Pennsylvania Germans have a word for this seemingly extraordinary behavior: *Gelassenheit.* It means the ongoing ability to let things go and live in the moment. It means relinquishing our cares and concerns and rolling with the punches life deals us without regret or rancor. It means relaxing into the circumstances we have at the time.

It is indeed a spiritual virtue, because it cannot be done without spiritual resources. Most of us get quite angry when things do not go right in our lives. We fuss and fume and lose our cool over even minor matters, like losing a parking space to the guy in front of us or breaking a wooden spoon.

For my mother and my friend's mother, who were faithful Christians, the whole thing traced back to Jesus. After all, it was he who said, "Do not take thought for the morrow, for the morrow shall take care of itself. Sufficient unto each day is the evil thereof."

Let us be present where we are. Accept the conditions of our life, whether foul or fair. If they are foul, let us deal with them as best we can. If we cannot understand the lesson of difficult times, we will wait patiently and it will be revealed to us.

My mother was an orphan at six and lost her guardian at thirteen. Life was never easy for her. But she lived by the virtue of *Gelassenheit*, including during the time when my father died abruptly when he was still relatively young. "Teach me to drive," she said, "I'm not going to spend the rest of my life in the house." By letting go, she was able to move on. No dwelling in the past. No whining about difficult times. Only pressing on toward the newness of the next day.

God is waiting if only we do not hold back and try to hold on to what has already gone by.

Memory, Meaning, and the Present Moment

Memory is able to bring a scene back to us in full-blown colors, textures, and voices. The tiniest article from the scene is enough to recreate the whole. It is as if we were watching a special effects movie in which an entire city silently emerges from nothingness.

In his book *Poetry and Experience*, the poet Archibald MacLeish wrote, "Poetry is a labor which undertakes to 'know' the world not by exegesis or demonstration of proofs but directly, as a man knows apple in his mouth." This knowledge can unfold in retrospect as well as in the present; the taste of an apple can bring back a whole picture from our memory.

For example, consider the lowly soup cracker. Rather, consider a specific soup cracker (for all memory is specific and detailed) that is called an OTC. That stands for "Original Trenton Cracker," after the factory that originally made them in Trenton, New Jersey. They are hard to find in New Mexico where we live, but they remain readily available on the East Coast. Every time I return there I want to buy some bags and bring them back with me.

So what is so important about the OTC? For me, that soup cracker brings back an entire experience. When I was a boy, on Friday nights in fall and winter my mother would host her bridge club at our house in Philadelphia. My father and I would abandon the premises to the ladies and go to a small seafood restaurant on Rising Sun Avenue. I would order oyster stew every time. While we waited for it to arrive, there were bowls of OTCs on the table that we would coat with horseradish and eat before our meal, to pique our appetites. The entire scene blossoms in my head as I recall it. You probably have scenes like this in your memory as well.

Often the most important things we have experienced in life are shrouded in memory. It takes but a nudge for them to burst into consciousness once again. More important than the mental picture, however, is the feeling that goes with it. Although they are buried beneath the surface, special times with relatives and friends live on in our consciousness. When triggered, they pop up again to put a smile on our face and bring a sense of warmth and wholeness to our psyche.

In fact, this is the very the reason that holidays often do not fulfill our expectations. They recede behind the idealized memories we make of past times. If you were only ten years old when you had the best Christmas you can ever remember, then it is hard to set the memory aside and revel in the present experience. In fact, that old memory only gets bigger and better with age.

But here is the problem: this is not memory. This is nostalgia, that wistful yearning for a past time that, in fact, never existed quite as we recall it. Truth is, the oyster stew of my youth was sometimes ruined by arguments my father and I had about my teenaged behavior, or by holding onto outside issues which prevented us from being present with each other.

So yes, go ahead and recall the great days of singing "Chestnuts Roasting on an Open Fire," or the year you got that special doll or chemistry set. But also remember that the present is ultimately all we have. This moment is real time. The present is our present, our gift. Memory can bring good feelings about what we deem golden times, but we cannot afford to let it rob us of the present moment. This, only, is the moment in which we find that Presence which fills life with meaning.

On High, Contemplating One World at a Time

Here I sit, on a rock on a mountain. The cawing crows and squawking Steller's Jays, the chatter of chipmunks scampering across the path, the tattoo of white-headed woodpeckers on a distant tree, the hooting of a solitary owl: all this would be symphony enough. But there is more. A nuthatch creeps down the bark of a Jeffrey pine searching for insects in the crevices. Here at seven thousand feet, where the air is thin and sound carries easily, the voices of people at a distance are distinctly audible.

The clarity of light at this elevation is mesmerizing. Trees are sharply delineated, distinct from one another in their majesty. Everything from an insect to a mountain is illuminated and magnified. The fly on the back of my hand as I write is not a pest, but a beautiful iridescent flying machine.

I have come away to rest, but in some ways there is too much activity here for that. This mountain world is a busy place filled with incessant wonders. Work and love are the foundation stones. I am reminded of the former and see the visible effects of the latter as twenty quail cross the road in search of pickings.

I remember a quote from Pearl Buck: "I am so absorbed in the wonder of earth and the life upon it that I cannot think of heaven and the angels. I have enough for this life."

The slower pace of life on holiday enables contemplation and introspection. We look outward to behold the wonders of creation, but we also look inward. We are stripped to the basics, and all is well.

The slow pace also encourages relationships. We see others in our sphere with greater clarity and depth, just as we see so-called objects which are separate from us.

Whatever it is that the structures and symbols, the rituals and regalia of religion point to (like the finger pointing at the moon in the Zen proverb), it becomes silently audible and invisibly evident up here at seven thousand feet.

My eyes rise another six hundred feet up the hillside, and I am one with the Psalmist who wrote, "I lift up my eyes to the mountains whence comes my help. From whence does my help come? My help comes from the Lord who made heaven and earth" (Psalm 121). Whatever those verses may mean to us, because of our belief in God or the absence thereof, they are meant to tell us that the universe is not as hostile as we may think. We inhabit a place where room can be made for us, and it may even bring warmth and succor.

Julian of Norwich, the 14th century British nun, lived in a century of plague, pestilence, famine, and seemingly endless war. It was as harsh as hell. Julian herself suffered illness nearly to the point of death when she was a young woman of thirty. In her contemplative years she saw lessons in the little stuff of nature. The hazelnut was an icon to her. From this little nut in her palm she drew three lessons: God made it, God loves it, and God will preserve it. If so small a thing is fashioned thus, how much more are we?

So I find that Pearl Buck's comment rings true, at least for me, and at this time. No need to go beyond the present moment or place to another realm. This one affords enough wonder, enough transcendence. One realm at a time. Just behold the hazelnut …or that hummingbird who just buzzed by … or that loving touch on your hand.

Biking, Meditation, and Attentiveness

My fellow bicyclists and I discuss many things while riding. One memorable conversation was when I clued them in to the over-age-sixty-five biking mantra, "Never fall." The behavior is even more important than the mantra.

It is true. At our age, lose attention for a nanosecond and we can lose our balance and hit the ground hard. So we learn that some activities require close attention.

There is a lesson in this – it is about the correlation between cycling and meditation. Just like riding our bikes, meditation is also all about paying attention. Lose concentration for a split second, and boom! We have hit the ground hard, metaphorically speaking. Anyone who has ever tried to enter into deep prayer and meditation knows that the very minute we start, all manner of uninvited thoughts begin to intrude upon our mind. This is the meditative counterpart of losing attention while riding.

To stay focused on one thing: that is the idea. But how hard it is to pull it off. There are all manner of distractions that occur. The minute we think that we are riveted in the moment, there is dinner to consider, or what were those people talking about on the street corner, or when am I going to finish that book that I am halfway through? These thoughts, like a logjam in the river that is our mind, are often so thick and numerous that we cannot see the water any more.

In an earlier age, we would have said that these are demons assailing us, trying to drive us away from our purpose. Maybe so; we need some way of naming what is going on here. Most of us would not choose to blame demons, but the distractions are surely, well, demonic, aren't they?

So let us approach distractions to meditation as if we were cycling. It works, and here is how. When we ride out the first five or six miles, we have distractions aplenty. Then suddenly, we simply begin to ride. We might even say "there is riding." We are unaware that we are working because it seems effortless. Time falls away; we are in the moment. When obstacles appear, we notice them but do not concentrate on them. We pay attention to them all, but the moment we pass them, they are gone.

Meditation works the same way. Here is a Zen story as illustration: two monks are walking a mountain path and come upon a quick-running stream where a woman stands on the bank, trying to cross. One monk, without thinking, hikes up his robe, picks her up, crosses the stream, and deposits her on the other side. Two miles down the road the other monk says, "I thought we were supposed to have nothing to do with women," to which the first monk replies, "I put her down two miles back. Why are you still carrying her?"

When we meditate, as when we cycle, we should let things go as quickly as we pass them by, or they pass us by. If we concentrate on the stuff we see or hear in our head – thoughts, ideas, opinions, even concepts of God – we lose focus on the moment, and we are bound to fall. Falling takes only a split second. In that split second, one thought can control us and take us out of the present. We need to allow meditation to happen in the same way that, when we are out a number of miles, cycling suddenly happens. Then there we are: fully present.

Many prayer masters tell us that this is the time that bears eternity, the moment that encompasses the universe. We can, and perhaps should, let all else pass us by. Be present in this moment, and we will know the Presence.

Bicycling and The Cosmic Christ

So much that passes for spirituality is dissociated from ordinary life. I have no idea where to lay the blame for this, but it is clear to me that many people believe that Christianity is in this dissociated camp.

Dualism is the correct term for this. Stated simplistically, dualism says that on one hand is the world, on the other hand is God, and we cannot have one without giving up the other. Hymns known from childhood either created this split or communicated the faith in ambiguous ways that seemed to separate it from daily life. "I'm but a stranger here, heaven is my home," we sang.

True, the intent of such hymnody was to turn us from distorted passions, fleeting emotions, and overconfidence in worldly matters. The net result, however, may have been to make us think "God's in his heaven" and all's wrong with the world.

There is a better alternative: to see the holy in the ordinary, the transcendent in the momentary, vast infinity within the confines of place. In the Christian tradition, this is sometimes called "seeing the cosmic Christ." Its biblical roots are in the two letters, attributed to Paul, of Colossians and Ephesians. Throughout my life I have found these letters to be not only comforting, but also incisive and even thrilling.

The idea of the cosmic Christ came through loud and clear in the early church, particularly in the writings of St Irenaeus of Lyons, the second century divine of the church in Gaul (France). Even the offbeat Gospel of Thomas conveyed that the face of Christ is everywhere. In it, Christ says, "Split wood and I am there. Lift the rock and you will find me."

Every craftsman experiences the spiritual aspect of her craft. We begin to understand that the specific bears the universal. This rings true for me, personally. I have written about the spiritual aspects of baking and calligraphy; experiences with birding over the years have given me the same feeling. Today I am thinking of cycling – about which I have also written a number of articles. Here is a great quote from Anglo-Irish writer Iris Murdoch: "The bicycle is the most civilized conveyance known to man. Other forms of transport grow daily more nightmarish. Only the bicycle remains pure in heart."

"Pure in heart?" Isn't that from Jesus' Sermon on the Mount (Matthew 5-7)? Of course it is, and Iris Murdoch had a twinkle in her eye when she wrote that. Jesus' saying is, "Blessed are the pure in heart, for they shall see God."

Is Murdoch saying that we will see God when we cycle? We cannot be sure, but that seems to be the most likely meaning. The bicycle will, so to speak, transport us to where we can see God. It is about the wind, freedom, connection to earth, and human-friendly speed. Cars and trucks are conveyances: they get you where you have to go, they hold your gear when you work, they can be filled with stuff you haul. But with singular exceptions that have to do with the beauty of design or the dance of driving, they are, well, pedestrian. On the other hand, the exquisite design of the bicycle, the simple perfection of the diamond frame, the extraordinary engineering of an internal or derailleur gearing system: these things thrill the soul as well as satisfy the body.

Notice that the human dimension is precisely the dimension in which we discover the divine. So it is that all the little things of human life can bear the Presence of God to us. That is the secret to the cosmic Christ.

What to Do When the World is Running Down

My favorite Eighties band was The Police. Recall these lyrics from their 1980 album *Zenyatta Mondatta*: "When the world is running down, you make the best of what's still around." My friends and I often discussed the album and this song. It was a strange time in our history, and the song, along with others like "Canary in a Coal Mine," seemed to give it a name. At some point, however, we all come to realize that there is no "normal" time in history; every time is strange in its own way.

Today we hear so many warnings: global warming, terrorism, wars, drug cartels, murders. Is the world running down, as Sting wrote thirty years ago? Yes it is, and no it is not. It is, because there is always danger – some from the natural world, but most of it driven by human greed and villainy. And no, it is not, because there are always folks who are working on the edges, and even in the center, to make sure that we can get to yet one more period of safe breathing.

Genuine spiritual pathways enable us to recognize that, although such dualities are true on one level, they are not the final answer. We can say that the world is running down. We can also say that how we see the world is constantly changing. As we deepen in intelligence and spiritual insight, our perceptions change. We realize that how we see the world may not necessarily be how the world is.

How can we deepen in intelligence and insight? Faith used to be the assumed pathway. But for many people, traditional forms of faith no longer connect, or perhaps their symbolism no longer reaches people with the impact it once did. For them, the symbols seem to be masks rather than windows onto the Holy, which is unfortunate.

Both effort and work are necessary to walk a spiritual pathway. One contemporary problem is that most people are not willing to invest the necessary time. Since we are accustomed to instant gratification, we want instant knowledge. But spiritual insight does not work that way; it will not be instantly forthcoming.

The mystics of the church pierced the illusion that hides what is real from our eyes. That illusion convinces us that ego and pride are central; it drives us to greed and envy. Those mystics knew that graciousness and faith are found below the surface of our day-to-day lives if we allow ourselves to be moved off of the egotistical center we usually occupy. We must set passions aside, which means we have to stop lusting after things or people that we believe will fill the holes in our souls. We have to let go of the fantasy that there is a magic pill that will cure our problems. To those cured in his presence, Jesus said, "Rise and go; your faith has made you whole" (Luke 17:19).

What is the content of this healing faith? First, it is a dismantling of the illusions that govern our view of this world. Old hymns tried to express this: "What is this world to me; a vain and vaunted pleasure." Although this sounds old-fashioned, it bears a truth: you are not going to find out who you are by paying attention to the greed, pride, and lust you find yourself swimming in. Whatever it means to find eternity, it surely includes breaking free from time- and ego-bound issues that keep our focus small and narrow. It means waking up.

Secondly, the heart of this contemplative faith is attentiveness and awareness. Paying attention leads us into the center of the universe. The poet William Blake said it: "to see a universe in a grain of sand." Is the world running down? Yes. Is there hope? Yes.

4

SAINT GWENFREWI

NOVEMBER 3

CHAPTER 4

Stones

ST GWENFREWI

Medieval hagiography offered three kinds of commemorations of saints: basic lives, accounts of suffering (martyrdom), and miracle stories. St Gwenfrewi (St Winifred) of Wales is commemorated on all three levels. In an age and a place dominated by male saints, Gwenfrewi stands out as a model of alternate spirituality. Wedded to the land and to place, she dominates a geographical corner of the world little known outside Britain but eminently famous therein.

Gwenfrewi, who died around 650, was the child of a family connected to royalty and, as so often happened in those times, she desired to choose the monastic life and avoid marriage. This was one of the only pathways by which strong women could not only keep their independence, but also use their willfulness as the gift it could rightly be, were they not subject to male domination.

Gwenfrewi's tale is dramatic. Described as a beautiful young woman, she desired to rely not upon the power of her beauty, but to relinquish its potential in favor of a life of devotion to Christ. As it is told, when a local prince named Caradoc became a suitor, the virgin saint spurned him, insisting that she prefered death to the loss of her virginity. In a fit of rage, he decapitated her, upon which the earth opened and swallowed him into hell. Gwenfrewi's Uncle Beuno (who also became a prominent Welsh saint) recovered her head and healed her. A spring burst forth from the earth where her head first fell, creating a pool called Winifred's Well that remains to this day.

One of Gwenfrewi's hagiographers, John Mirk, prior of Lilleshall Abbey in Shropshire, tenderly relates the details following her miraculous resurrection at the hand of Beuno. He tells us that for seven years (a sign of perfection or wholeness), she remained at the well with Beuno, after which she embarked on a period of holy wandering, taking counsel with a series of holy men.

At last she entered the monastery at Gwytherin, where she ultimately became abbess. Finally established in this place, Gwenfrewi proved to be an excellent and sought-out spiritual counselor, as well as an astute and able administrator. According to the *Life* by Robert of Shrewsbury, she became known as White Winifred because "she discoursed with the radiance of wisdom," whiteness being equal to light and, hence, identified with spiritual illumination.

An icon of patience and obedience to her nuns, Gwenfrewi died after fifteen years at Gwytherin. In death she became even more famous than in life. People flocked to her grave to venerate her relics and receive healing from her, just as they had done when she was alive.

John Mirk tells us that the saint's original name was Brewafour. The name Gwenfrewi means "white thread," commemorating the scar where her head was rejoined to her neck. The scar is visible in statuary and icons of the saint.

As time passed, St Gwenfrewi's relics were venerated in several places. They finally came to rest at the Monastery of SS. Peter and Paul in Shrewsbury, a small city on the Severn River whose governance shifted back and forth between Wales and England in the middle ages. A delightful fictionalized, though historically accurate, account of her translation is told in Book 20 of *The Chronicles of Cadfael* by Ellis Peters.

The place at Winifred's Well, appropriately called Holywell, has been sought out since the seventh century and is the oldest continuously visited pilgrimage site in the British Isles. We remember St Gwenfrewi on November 3.

TROPAR

> *Suffering death for thy virginity,*
> *O Holy Winefride,*
> *Through God's mercy thy body was made whole*
>   *and restored to life.*
> *Thy healing grace flows in streams of living water.*
> *Pray to God for us,*
> *That our souls may be saved.*

Special Places: Their Crucial Role in Our Lives

My friend Bruce lives in rolling country twenty-three hundred miles away from me. To get to his home, we exit the interstate, go about seven miles on a four-lane state highway, turn onto a two-lane blacktop for six miles, dogleg onto a dirt road that rolls on for about a mile then dips down past a dairy farm and turns a sharp left along a creek, and there it is – a modernized cabin set back against a hill, walled in by hemlock, oak, and maple. Bruce's place has been special to me for years. It was once the parenthetical marks that enclosed my vacations, the first and last stops in the Chicago-to-Philadelphia loop.

Bruce's place is also special because it marked a different way of life from what I was living in the big cities of Philadelphia and Chicago. His place, which I fondly call "Rancho Deluxe," represents a pace, an environment, and a feeling that it is important to recall in times of stress and overdone populations. To put it simply, it is a spiritual oasis.

The way the herons, geese, and ducks populate the shores of the creek, the erratic flight of the bank swallows, the cry of the killdeer, the occasional green kingfisher flying upstream and diving: these create the spirit of the place.

Relationships are also important to the place. Bruce and I go back over forty years, and the quality of our conversation is always nourishing, challenging, and deep. Around his stove, a spiritual center binds us together along with the warmth of the fire. We know that we are not unique in this; special places enhance everybody's conversations.

When my children were young, I used to create special places for them to inhabit. They were not much: a corner of a room here, a nook there, with a children's library and a backrest for reading. We all went there to feel safe, to be comforted, to be together. We found security there against the winds of fortune that surrounded us.

We are promised a special place in the heart of God, but we often need the physical experience of special places to discover where that heart may be known. A creekside cabin. A tiny corner for children. A cathedral in France or Russia. An ancient adobe church on a hill. All of these are doorways into that larger heart that embraces and encompasses us all.

The special place may also be within us. Some of the early Christian teachers interpreted Jesus' words, "I go to prepare a place for you" to mean the Spirit's preparation of a special place in our own hearts to which we could return again and again, and in which we would be met by God. This special place is comforting and secure. Prayer marks our constant return to it, this "little chamber of the heart," as the 18th century teacher and hymn writer Gerhard Tersteegen called it. In our Orthodox tradition, we use the simple words, "Lord, have mercy," as a repeated form of prayer to bring us into our own hearts and into the heart of God, who is always waiting but so often kept waiting by our busy agendas.

So as we are moved to recall the special places that we hold dear, we can know that they are reminders of a more full and eternal special place that has been prepared for us and in which we may find refuge and safety. We will be challenged at the very core of our being there, as well, but we will find an underlying sense of affirmation that will not disappoint us.

Solitude in Open Spaces

I drive north on I-25 to Albuquerque or Santa Fe monthly. My eastern friends who have never been to the West or Southwest ask me, what is that like? To them, "out of doors" looks like dense forests and hills that go on forever. Even if they travel beyond the cities into the rural East, the vast panorama of New Mexico remains unimaginable to them, way beyond anything they have ever experienced.

Despite talk about America as a mobile society, I know many people who have never been farther west than Ohio and who think that Chicago is virtually the Far West. They may have flown over places like Kansas or Colorado, but they have never set foot on the soil or walked the ground. Similarly, people who have spent their entire lives in the Southwest probably cannot picture I-287 around New York City, a six-lane interstate highway with wall-to-wall traffic on which eighteen-wheelers roar along at 85 mph.

So what is I-25 like? I go north like an arrow out of the Mesilla Valley, and then it is wide open spaces with incredibly broad vistas and few houses until I hit Truth or Consequences. Then it is wide open spaces with broad vistas until I hit Socorro. And then … well, you get the idea. It is hard to describe the solitude and spaciousness driving on I-25 North through New Mexico, radio silent and only road hum in my ears. To see a panorama sixty miles across – it is beyond comprehension to my eastern friends. And I love it.

Like most kids, I sought out places of solace and solitude when I was young. This spiritual urge for a secret place that feels like it belongs just to us, our secret fort, castle, or refuge, seems to come early in life. We search for a place at once universal and yet specific, where time and eternity overlap, and we can find ourselves. Paradoxically, we feel a sense of community in the midst of solitude.

A small creek flowed not far from the house where I grew up. I tramped through fields of corn stubble and slid down a little embankment to reach the damp and cool water's edge. Muskrats scurried at my approach, and frogs galumphed as they splashed into the water. I usually had the place to myself. Would I say I knew God there? I do not know; I have always been reluctant to identify my experience of holiness as the presence of the divine. But it felt holy there, like a sanctuary, holier than the sanctuary of the church we attended in my little Pennsylvania town.

Beyond isolated creek banks, solitude can be found everywhere. Gretel Ehrlich wrote a reflection called *The Solace of Open Spaces* about life in Wyoming. In it, she celebrated the resources she found that are so necessary to us in what some may consider to be bleak landscapes. Henri Nouwen named the inner feel of these resources: "Without silence words lose their meaning, without listening speaking no longer heals, without distance closeness cannot cure. Somewhere we know that without a lonely place our actions quickly become empty gestures."

Solitude affords us the chance to drop out of competition, noisiness, and the need to respond to others. Many of us pass up the opportunity for solitude because we cannot bear silence. Instead, we seek refuge in noise or ceaseless chatter.

Solitude requires effort to regain the centering and quietude that many of us have lost in our restless world. But seek it, and rewards await us when we finally arrive. As Henri Nouwen knew, solitude demands and evokes true gestures and genuine speech. In New Mexico or in the solitude of any of our open spaces, we may find a presence we call God.

Seeing the Shook Foil of Creation

John Scotus Eriugena, the greatest wisdom teacher of the Celtic Christian world, taught that God wrote two books. The smaller of the two is the scriptures, which contain God's truth. But there is also a larger book of truth: the creation. Already in the ninth century Eriugena knew that we were losing our ability to read it.

Creation reveals God, and emphasis on that fact is one of the great gifts of the Celtic Christian world. George MacLeod, the 20th century rejuvenator of the Iona Community in Scotland, speaks of the "thin places." Standing there, the line between sacred and profane is blurred and in fact overcome; we know ourselves to be in a holy Presence.

In the 19th century, the poet-priest Gerard Manley Hopkins spoke of the universe as "shook foil" showing forth the grandeur of God. As a calligrapher and illuminator, I know about shook foil. Gold foil is so thin that, if held to the light, we can see through the sheet. It must be handled carefully; it is so light that the smallest breath will blow it and crinkle it onto itself. Gold foil reflects light as if it were illuminated from within. And so it is with the creation, if we can only see it. Ah, but there's the rub: *if* we can see it. Our vision has been clouded over by centuries of teaching that the creation is an inferior teacher to scripture.

Why have we lost the ability to see God in the creation? The church is at fault in many ways. Some key churchly teachings separated people from the earth and engrained in us the belief that matter is inferior to spirit. One teaching that underlies this split is that human sinfulness renders us totally helpless and bereft of any connection to God. This teaching, which drove a wedge between creation and God, was pervasive in much of the church. The ensuing sense of estrangement from God and his grace continues to drive many people from the church. We have not yet fully overcome it.

We have also lost the ability to see God in creation because of the teaching of some Christians that sexuality, and even creativity, are bad. They drew an erroneous line between spirit and matter, a line that unfortunately enabled those who wanted to exploit the earth to do so. People conveniently forgot that we are called to be stewards of the creation and not abusers of its resources.

Eriugena knew that, in the words of J. Philip Newell, "To listen to creation without scripture is to lose the cosmic vastness of the song. And to listen to scripture without creation is to lose the personal intimacy of the voice." The two belong together if we are to know our place in the sacred universe. One text addresses us personally, the other text addresses us physically. We need both of them for wholeness, just as our body cannot be whole without our soul.

Once, while cycling, I saw a burrowing owl along our new city path. We looked at each other and knew a deep oneness as interrelated parts of the creation. I am not apart from the creation, nor from the burrowing owl, nor, for that matter, from the lazuli bunting I spotted in flight later.

As farmer-philosopher Wendell Berry puts it, we are not apart from, but we are a part of, the creation. We are one in that spiritual matter that God created. Recovering this awareness, we will recover a deeper sense of the church's call to oneness. This call to oneness is much bigger than a call to overcoming the rift between religions. We are called to recognize and live our union with all creation. That is the way that leads to healing.

Courting the Rebirth of Wonder

Poet Lawrence Ferlinghetti wrote, "I am awaiting the rebirth of wonder." We know wonder at the birth of a child, in outpourings of unselfish love in tragic times, and when we meet old friends. In our daily round, however, we tend to forget how wonder-filled our lives are. Our noses are too near the grindstone to look out, our shoulders too hunched to the wheel to feel anything but the weight.

"The world is charged with the grandeur of God," wrote Gerard Manley Hopkins. Hopkins' vision did not overlook the pain in the world. Instead, he knew that we can bind up some, if not all, of that pain when we approach the world in a spirit of wonder. Seeing a world charged with the grandeur of God, he knew eternity in the midst of time, the limitless within the limited.

Hopkins discovered the extraordinary in the ordinary, the boundless in the limited, and the eternal in the daily. Truly, the best place to look for universals is in particulars. We may declare in noble tones that we love humanity; the problem is that we cannot stand our next-door neighbor. To love the particular is far more difficult. We are called to love *this* neighbor, or *this* child, or *this* spouse, not a universal idea. Wonder greets us in the ordinary, the daily, in this particular person who stands before us and confronts us in all of her magnificent otherness.

In the second century, St Irenaeus wrote, "the glory of God is a person, fully revealed." That great saint had a handle on the truth. Humanity is not a given, it is a calling. We might even call it an achievement. And we are called to assist one another to become fully human. We celebrate the triumph of wonder over cynicism, of joy over pessimism. There are so many wounded people in our sphere who no longer live in wonder; more often than not, that includes us, ourselves.

Further exploring Irenaeus' statement that the glory of God is a fully revealed person, we see yet another way that he had it right. The Hebrew word for glory means weight, in the sense of deep importance, or full presence, or impressive dignity. If we have a gentle spirit, we invite others to reveal themselves more fully, to open up their weightiness in our presence. We, in turn, may reveal our full human weight in their presence. In this way, we become really present one to another. Just so is wonder reborn.

In doing this, we may need to use discretion. My old friend, the psychologist and theologian Robert Moore, told me, "You have to be careful to whom you show your gold, because the world is full of people who cannot see the wonder of another person any more. They will squash you." For these poor souls, their supply of wonder is so depleted that they negate, rather than affirm, others. They have become toxic; they would rather poison the water than to drink it. They want to drag us down to their level rather than meet us on the one we occupy. We know who they are. Sadly, they may even be in our families.

Nevertheless, wonder surrounds us. The word "God" may throw us, but we know at heart a sense of the sacredness of life, however fleeting it may be – as fleeting as the wind in autumn whispers the leaves past your face. Even if we cannot hold it, we can touch that wonder. Like the chickadee that lights on our hand to take seed on a winter day, so is the time of wonder. If we try to close our hand, it will fly away.

Let us rejoice at the rebirth of wonder wherever we find it, and give thanks.

Living Lightly Upon the Earth

I cannot remember a time when I was unconcerned about my environment, wilderness, and the natural world. It made sense to me: if we affirm a Creator, what is more logical than loving the creation? Because of our relationship to God as our loving Creator, we are called to be responsible stewards of the creation.

The challenge of stewardship has been with us since the beginning. Adam and Eve, so to speak, had to deal with trash simply because they occupied space and used the resources available to them. Others may approach these issues from other perspectives, but as Christians we seek to find a balance between abuse and restraint; we seek to understand what it means to be within, and not outside of, the created universe and order.

True, the concern that Christians and other people of faith have for the environment cannot prevent such natural phenomena as forest fires, flooding, or long-term drought. But at the very least, a sense of responsibility for nature as a spiritual calling might lead to greater consciousness about, and better use of, resources. For instance, we might question the business of packaging that has grown to monumental proportions in the USA. Might there be some way to lessen this excess? We might also question the amount and the quality of the food we consume.

In the late 1970s, many of us were asking questions like these and trying to develop alternatives; we called it "voluntary simplicity." Even those of us who were urban dwellers committed to making at least some small difference through the adoption of simpler ways of living. For many of us this meant walking or biking to market rather than driving. But we quickly realized that for every move we made in the direction of simplicity, the culture – and specifically the culture of business – was advancing further into the reaches of complexity, overuse, and, well, packaging. It seemed to be a losing battle.

If we believe that our God-given role is to be part of the creation, to some extent *participants* in creation, and to live and move and have our being enmeshed in the creation, do we not have a responsibility to live as lightly upon the earth as we can? I feel it in my own soul. Not a week goes by without my noticing the amount of trash our one small house of two or three people produces, despite our efforts to recycle and reuse. I wonder, can it be reduced even more? These concerns arise automatically in the consciousness of those who claim to be faithful and responsible. We are, in a profound way, our brother's and sister's keepers. That means that we do not have the right to abuse the space we share.

This profound loss of connection to our natural setting, and to one another, is a spiritual problem. It has wreaked havoc not only with our habitat, but also with our minds. We have become lonely aliens in a world with which we no longer have an intimate connection.

How did this happen? We began to lose our conscience, along with our consciousness, back when we began to perceive the natural realm primarily as a resource to be used up. This lack of connection to our setting allows for a posture of domination. But we are, in fact, interconnected; this calls us to responsible interaction.

Finding our proper place in creation once again is a spiritual issue. What pathways might we take to recognize that we are a part of the creation, rather than apart from it? What one practical step might we take today that will affirm this connection?

Home is Everywhere: The Celtic Way

To be at home everywhere – on earth, with others, in various languages: this is a major aspect of the Celtic spirit. Unfortunately, much of what passes for Christian teaching goes in an opposite direction. "Flee the world which would deceive us," warned one of the hymns of my youth. Don't do this; don't do that: the spirit of negativity surrounds us. A world-affirming spirit, however, invites us into a universe that shouts holy everywhere and lets us see our conversations as evoking that Word which informs every word. So where is that world-affirming Celtic spirit when we need it most?

It is difficult to live in the spirit that finds us at home, everywhere. Our path is strewn with obstacles. Particularly as westerners, we long ago divided the world into body and soul. And as my father would say, soul takes the hindmost; it gets little support and not much nourishment.

Of course the division itself is the problem. That is the initial answer to where the world-affirming Celtic spirit has gone. That world-affirming spirit needs a world-affirming human to show it forth. But when we split body from soul, we rob ourselves of the ability to affirm the whole because we ourselves are no longer whole. To be materialistic is not to be world-affirming, it is to magnify one aspect of life at the loss of what most sages throughout history knew was more foundationally important: the spiritual.

Lest the reader jump to the conclusion that I am denying the material at the expense of the spiritual, let me hasten to shout, No! What I am after, and what the Celtic tradition exhibits again and again in ordinary people as well as in the saints, is a vision and understanding that the world is a spiritual-material realm; one cannot be denied without detriment to the other. But there is a natural order which the Celts understood: the spiritual is the source, the ground, the fountain of the material. It is also the glue that holds the material world together.

This understanding was quite locally focused for the Celts; there are significant places all over the Celtic world that hold the promise of sanctity, holiness, and the special presence of God - as if they were sacraments. Lindisfarne, the Holy Island, is one, and so is Croagh Patrick, and Solsbury Hill, and Holywell, and Bardsey Island off the coast of Wales. Each of these places discloses a unified reality of spirit and matter.

The poet William Blake spoke out of that same tradition

when he said that we could see the universe in a grain of sand. And the spiritual friend Julian of Norwich spoke out of that tradition when she said that the hazelnut could reveal to us the goodness of God wherein "all things would be well." We do not have to be Irish or Welsh, in other words, to attain this spiritual vision. It is available to all of us.

If we concentrate on the ordinary, and reflect on the uniqueness of all things, then we will discover the extraordinary in the object of our focus. It could be a morning sunrise, an evening sunset, the hands of our child, the peculiar way our dog tilts its head at the sound of our voice. The spiritual is there just below the surface, shining through, resplendent with glory.

Jesus affirms this vision for us when he says that God knows every hair of our head, and sees the sparrow fall from the tree.

In the *Black Book of Carmarthen*, a Welsh manuscript from about 1250, a Christian poet writes: "I praise the One ... who is God himself. He made Mars and Luna, man and woman, the difference in sound between shallow water and the deep ...." Note well that final phrase. The poet's ear is so finely-tuned that he hears the difference in water as a manifestation of the Holy. That is the world-affirming spirit. May it be ours, as well.

Bypassing our Destination

My friend the poet Wally Swist writes, "We're in such a hurry that we miss our real destinations." Our real destination is rigorous and demanding before it becomes enlightening and comfortable. Lost in our hurrying, we hurry on by. Like the white rabbit in Alice in Wonderland, we are always late for a date we have forgotten. And we do not claim the space that is rightfully ours to inhabit.

"Faith comes by hearing," says St Paul in his letter to the Romans. That is true. We begin with the community proclamation of the message. However, Christian faith then leads to a new vision of the world as it alters our perception through the vigor of the resurrection. It alters our perception of the places we inhabit with our presence; indeed, it expands our presence so that we fill up our places and spaces with the light of the resurrection.

This vigor is robust and deep and thoughtful. Justin the Martyr, a second-century church father, wrote about his exploration of the philosophies of his time. Justin says that a flame was kindled in his mind when he recognized that all the philosophies were best understood in the light of the gospel of Christ. What a memorable phrase: *a flame in the mind.* What a powerful image. The gospel illuminates our understanding and possesses glory weightier than fleeting emotions, more stable than decaying relationships. The gospel also burns up the dross of our minds, the collective, accumulated thoughts that, in the end, don't add up to a hill of beans.

Swist goes on to say, "We need to remember to return to the source whose center can be referenced anywhere." For Christians the source is the Easter Mystery. Not a once-a-year thing, mind you, but weekly, daily, minute-by-minute. Weekdays are transformed when we live out the power of our meeting with God the Risen Lord that we experience on Sundays. The message of resurrection constantly ignites our minds and transforms our hearts.

The transformed heart is born when we know this extraordinary love shown to us: "God became human in order that humanity might partake of Godliness." That saying fueled the Christian movement from earliest times and it burns at the heart of our message still today.

Justin's illumination of the mind may come in flashes or in a blinding light. The fire is kindled at Easter in the blaze of glory that is the Resurrection of Christ, who came "trampling down death by death and on those in the tombs bestowing life." The holy fire comes from the sepulcher and spreads to the entire world.

Easter is the night of baptism, when neophytes are illumined with the light of Christ, who enlightens the whole world. On this night the whole church shines with light, and it is the time when we remember our real destination. This night we rest at the center of our faith. We look out from this center onto a world transformed by God's love and grace. Gerard Manley Hopkins once again reminds us that "all creation is like shook foil," and it shines with the brightness of God's holy and compassionate presence. This is the night when the mind may be ignited.

Our world is so often bleak, desperate, and terrifying. Wars continue. Children die. Murders are committed. Faithfulness departs. There is much darkness; there is not much light. Christian faith is not Pollyanna, but it *is* promise. There is light at the end of the tunnel – the light of the cross and the resurrection, in and through which God proposes to "make all things new." The message of the resurrection drives us more deeply into the world with a vision for its healing, and a heart willing to work toward that end. That vision must take root in the very place where we find ourselves, for it too is holy ground.

The Spirituality of Place: Closing Thoughts

Think about the thin places, as they are called in the Celtic realm, those places where the lines between this world and the next, time and eternity, are blurred and overlapping.

If you have some background in biblical studies you will likely think of thin places recorded within those pages as well. Think of the bush that burned but was not consumed, where Moses sheds his sandals because he is on holy ground. Think of Mount Sinai, covered in cloud and smoke, where Moses meets God and receives the commandments. Remember Elijah who, seeking the presence of the Lord, is told that he will not find it in all the noise and clangor. Instead, he finds it in the "still, small voice" which, in Hebrew, reads as "the voice of silence." Remember Isaiah in the Temple, having the vision of God "high and lifted up," surrounded by the seraphim. Remember Ezekiel with his vision of wheels within wheels.

No, thin places are not limited to the Celtic realms. In fact, they have precedents in the hallowed pages of that book which was so central to genuine Celtic spirituality.

It may be, however, that within the Celtic realms it is most evident that there are, indeed, places where we can taste and touch holiness, where eternity pierces the veil of time. I myself have felt this on Lindisfarne, the Holy Island, off the north-west coast of England. I have felt the thinness while standing at St Cuthbert's tomb, past the lion's head pulls on the gates of Durham Cathedral. I have known the thin places in a wonderful megalith park, a magical place called Columcille outside Bangor, Pennsylvania. I have known thin places on the top of a hill in the Ring of Kerry where, for a moment, it was impossible to distinguish between earth and heaven.

To this day, Winifred's Well remains a thin place for pilgrims from all over, but especially from within the British Isles. Melangell's sanctuary in North Wales gives the same sort of experience. There is something special about the sanctity of a place that has been touched by those who bear the mark of Christ.

For Americans, there are places close to hand like Chaco Canyon and the kivas of the pueblos. Elsewhere, people continue to journey to Machu Picchu, Angkor Wat, and Hagia Sophia to experience the transcendence that accompanies such monuments. It is not merely antiquity that sheathes these spots in silent reverie; there is a holiness of place that we often miss in our hustle-and-bustle, tear it down and build it anew, society.

Perhaps the most obvious thin place, for those of us within the great tradition of the church's faith, is the altar where Christ becomes real to us in the bread and wine of the Eucharist. Truly the altar is the *axis mundi* – the still point of the turning world where matter takes on spirit once again, where time crosses into eternity, and where the enclosed space of the sanctuary opens onto the panoply of the heavens – angels, archangels, seraphim and all present with us. "Oh taste and see that the Lord is good. . . ." The words of Psalm 33 echo in our hearts as well as resound on our tongues as we continue to discover the depth in the sacrament.

We owe gratitude to our Celtic forebears for keeping the awareness of thin places alive. Their testimony rings true to this day. Let us find our own thin places, returning to them physically if possible, or if not, let us do so in contemplation.

5

SAINT HILDA

NOVEMBER 17

CHAPTER 5

Spirit

ST HILDA

The story is told of a little girl who, standing in an Orthodox church, was asked if she knew who the saints were. Looking at the icons on the walls and screen, she said, "The saints are people who let in the light." So it was with St Patrick, St Aidan, St David, St Ninian, St Ita, St Hilda, and many more Celtic saints who illuminated the islands known today as Great Britain with the gospel.

Although these Celtic saints were likely unaware of it, they were caught up in a significant moment of church history, a hinge of history when, in the seventh century, the Roman Church was expanding its influence westward. St Hilda played a significant part in that story.

Born in Northumbria of noble parents in 614, Hilda grew up firm in the faith. Her mother had had a dream that her daughter would become a shining light to the nation, and so she was. For once Hilda found her true calling in life, she shone forth with brilliance to those around her, both intellectually and spiritually.

When St Aidan, now Bishop Aidan of Lindisfarne, arrived in Northumbria, Hilda left her inheritance and became a nun there. She eventually became Abbess of Whitby in 657.

Hilda was a great administrator who developed a rule for the community, which included both men and women. Under her leadership, Whitby became a center for learning, literature, and the arts, a university before the rise of such academies. For in those days, all people could attend these schools for study and learning, not only the clergy or monastics.

Bede the Venerable, chronicler of the early church in the British Isles, said of Hilda that she was full of virtues; his list includes justice, devotion, chastity, peace, and love. She was so deeply imbued with the Spirit of Christ that she exuded peace and love. This attracted many to her monastery and to the faith.

In 664, an important ecclesiastical gathering ("synod") was held at Whitby. Hilda hosted this gathering, which was called to chart the future development of the Church in the British Isles. Colman, Abbot of Lindisfarne; Cedd, Bishop of Anglia; and Hilda all argued that the Celtic Church should maintain mutual respect with, but autonomy from, Rome. Wilfrid, Bishop of Ripon, argued that it would be better to go with Roman administration for the sake of the unity of the Church. His view won the day; unity's cause was nobly served.

The Whitby Synod was indeed a hinge of history. After the Synod of Whitby, the Celtic Church began to wane across the British Isles and, eventually, its witness was subsumed under that of Rome. Practically speaking, this meant the end of independent monasteries (such as Whitby), as the Roman Rule, which made monastic life less flexible and spontaneous, came into place. Faith became more intellectual, less earthy. The loss has not yet been overcome in the West.

We boldly include St Hilda's name in the list of those who let in the Light of Christ. In these days when there seems to be tension, even hostility, between learning and faith, the witness of St Hilda is a shining beacon for a deeply intellectual faith that satisfies both soul and mind. She remains an exemplar of one lit by the Holy Spirit even unto our day. We remember St Hilda of Whitby on November 17.

TROPAR

Though thou wast of royal birth and lineage,
    O Hilda,
Thou didst spurn earthly riches and the allure-
    ments of the flesh.
And cleaving with all thy heart unto Christ,
Thou didst take up the struggle of the monastic
    life.
Wherefore, God endowed thee with such wisdom
    and prudence,
That all the people hastened unto thee for counsel
    and succour.
O Venerable One, entreat Him unceasingly,
That He grant us great mercy.

Choosing Between Rejection and Inclusion

Jesus leaps off the pages of the gospel as many different persons. Among his different *personae*, we see a teacher of wisdom in the Jewish sense, one who contemplates life from various angles and offers his insights in pithy saying and wise parables. Other times, he utters paradoxical statements that sound like nonsense, statements that we understand by insight rather than by logic. In this regard he sounds like teachers from other arenas, like Zen Buddhism. When his words echo the Psalms or Proverbs of old, with which he was so familiar, he can sound like teachers of the Eastern traditions of Confucianism and Taoism.

I am always surprised when I meet Christians – and I have to say it is usually Christians – who reject insights from other wisdom teachers. It seems that their sense of commitment to Jesus rules out any appreciation of other teachers. For them, if their attention is not given to Jesus exclusively, they feel disloyal or unfaithful.

I disagree with that approach. Instead, I believe that we can embrace Jesus and still be open, even welcoming, to insights from other sages. I have read Stephen Mitchell's *Second Book of the Tao*, based mostly on the writings of Chuang Tzu, a "crazy wisdom" teacher of ancient China.

Mitchell's Chuang Tzu hammers home two main points. First, since it is impossible to fully comprehend the meaning of life, why not just live it as it comes without trying to control it? Therefore, yielding is preferable to confrontation. Acceptance is more healthy than opposition. Second, though we cannot fully understand life, what is clear is that we understand nothing without contrasts. We don't know good without evil, right without wrong, light without dark. We note that these are not, however, total opposites. Each contains, in some measure, the other.

Does this sound abstract? Not so. For Chuang Tzu, it is a way of life. And if we turn to Jesus, we see these truths enacted in his mission, also. For in the Israel of Jesus' time, much energy was put into making distinctions between people. Folks related to the ones who were considered worthy, or, to use the appropriate word, holy.

In contrast, Jesus follows a path of inclusion, not rejection. His ministry embraces high and low, rich and poor, good and bad, all sorts of people who exemplify these contrasts. Instead of shunning those considered bad, he includes them at his table. He surrounds himself with tax collectors, prostitutes, and "sinners" – those who were rejected by the standard-bearers of the day. Most of us would have been too discriminating for his taste.

Today it is this sense of discrimination, which is actually a lack of compassion, that so often turns people away from the churches that bear Jesus' name. They have a sense of being unworthy, of being "unholy," to the point where they are sure that they cannot fit in, and they turn away.

What is this incessant need we have to divide people on the basis of external characteristics? Is it our inner lack of security that makes us invent such distinctions and puff ourselves up? When we feel inadequate or insecure in our own bodies, we tend to become less accepting toward others. When we work to make ourselves look better in our own eyes and, we hope, in the eyes of others, it leads to a false sense of elevation. But that feeling dissolves with time, so we have to continually find new and other ways to distinguish ourselves from the pack.

Chuang Tzu's approach to this problem is clear, though it may be puzzling to those who spend their lives in rejection and opposition. "The Master lives in the center; the immature live on the edge of things, unsatisfied, always reaching for what is not. The Master lives in harmony; the immature pick and choose, accept some things and reject some, making themselves miserable trying to control the world." As for Jesus, check out these words: "If you love only those who love you, what reward can you expect? … There must be no limit to your goodness, as your heavenly Father's goodness knows no bounds." Live at peace, my friends. Let us use our commitment not for rejection, but for inclusion.

Follow the Wild Goose to Freedom

In the beginning … a great wind blew over the waters in the midst of nothingness. That is how the Book of Genesis begins. Later on we hear the wind blowing through the land and resting on special chosen people. Throughout the Old and New Testaments we hear this wind. We usually call it the Holy Spirit to indicate that the wind comes from God and, in a truth that we cannot fully grasp, *is* God.

The dove symbolizes this Spirit in the imagery of the New Testament. During the period following Epiphany (January 6) we Orthodox bless houses. Going from room to room, we sing a hymn of "the Spirit, in the form of a dove," referring to the picture from the Gospels when Christ was baptized.

As Christian faith spread through the British Isles, the Irish, the Welsh, and the Scots were brought into the fold. In particular, St Columba was influential in founding monasteries (which were educational institutions) beginning from his base on the island of Iona off the northwest coast of Scotland. Columba, though Irish, bore a Latin name that means "dove." Through odd changes in Celtic languages, dove became *paloma* in Spanish and Galician.

On the ancient wind-blown heath of western Scotland, the rough coasts of Ireland and Wales, and the tidal waters of Lindisfarne, the dove was too tame a symbol for the experience of the Celtic people. They found another avian image for their experience of the Spirit: the wild goose.

Geese are notoriously feisty. They bite people; they honk loudly and nip at our ankles if we get too close. Not the friendliest animals, they are quite different from doves, which seem so passive and calm.

It must have been the way the Spirit shook the peoples of the western Celtic lands that caused this switch from dove to goose. Their native tendency to restlessness resembled the geese that fly off for migration, return, then fly off again. This restlessness was enshrined in the idea of "white martyrdom," the practice of going abroad to found a church or a monastery, an outpost of the faith. This is how Christianity reached the western borders of Europe at the Atlantic Ocean and bounced back onto the mainland. Columbanus, another dove-named monk, followed the wild goose in freedom and established monasteries in France and Italy.

Jesus spoke of the freedom of the Spirit, and that Spirit blew steadily throughout the Celtic church in the early centuries. That mighty wind inspired creative approaches to ministry, to organization, and to faith itself.

There is more. Wild geese fly high, on one hand, and come low to earth in flocks on the other. In the image of the goose, we see heaven and earth come together in a way that is characteristic of Celtic Christianity. Welsh priest A. M. Allchin points out that the best Welsh poetry shows this spiritual unity between heaven and earth, so that earth and heaven are no longer two, but one in the Spirit. We sense this unity at crossing points like sacred hills and wells.

Monks and geese establish outposts far away, then return again whence they came. Listen as Mary Oliver – a poet who often uses avian imagery - expresses this unity of earth and heaven, geese and people, local and universal:

Whoever you are, no matter how lonely,
The world offers itself to your imagination,
Calls to you like the wild geese, harsh and exciting –
Over and over announcing your place
In the family of things.

The Tension Between Form and Spirit

Newspaper reports have noted that Protestantism has dropped below majority status in the U.S. In the fine print, the articles also say that all religions are experiencing diminished numbers. This may be because commitments to any broad organization are also way down. This change raises the age-old issue of "organized religion." What is actually happening to people, that they are avoiding commitment to organized religion?

One of the things people struggle with in faith is to find the balance between Spirit and form. The Spirit blows where it wills, as Jesus said, and no one can predict its whereabouts. From the Spirit's activity, an organization inevitably grows to give form and substance to the Spirit.

Then, when form is opposed to Spirit, tension rises. Change agents, innovators, and creative forces all work toward encouraging outpourings of the Spirit. Keepers of the flame, conservators, and guardians all work to preserve the organism that bears the Spirit. Frequently they come into tension.

As a priest of the church, I recognize and understand this tension. Therefore I strive to conserve a tradition that offers the essence of faith from generation to generation – without strangling the Spirit. Regarding the tradition, I am mystified by those who act as if there was no church between Pentecost and, say, the 16th century. Tradition is simply the form the Spirit takes in the church. As church historian Jaroslav Pelikan famously said, "Traditionalism is the dead faith of the living; Tradition is the living faith of the dead."

Orthodox Christianity, my faith tradition, is committed to the fullness of the faith, which involves gestures and the use of the senses, and historic patterns of worship and interpretation of scripture. These things enable people to experience faith beyond simply thinking about it or claiming to be believers. They are intended to keep form and Spirit in balance. That is why we Orthodox believe that ideas need time to prove themselves right, that we should wait before changing things, that discretion is the better part of valor. We live by the old axiom that whoever marries the Spirit of the Age will be quickly widowed. Perhaps this is why we have experienced only one major division in our history.

It is also true that forms and structures may block or hamper communication. Put bluntly, some rules and regulations get in the way of people seeing what the church offers to the world. Nevertheless, conservation has its merits, and history seems to show that they outweigh the disadvantages.

For instance, observe the growth of the multiple divisions and fragmentations in Christianity. Reformer after reformer has tried to "get it right," "to start over," "to return to the New Testament Church" and so forth, only to fail to achieve the unity they sought to restore. Nor have those who tried to reduce the elements to some imagined or proposed bottom line of faith had lasting success.

There are always those who want to re-invent the wheel. Truth to tell, the next generation will consolidate and organize the thrust of the re-inventors. And by the third generation there will be those calling again for reform, opposed to those who hold the, by now, "sacred trust." We have seen this cycle so often throughout history you would think we would get the message. But we do not.

Try as we might, we cannot escape the tension between organization and creativity, between form and Spirit. It cannot be overcome by denying it. We can only overcome the tension by embracing it, by making it an ongoing part of our life together.

Both sides are of good will here. No one denies the freedom of the Spirit to lead in new directions. If we lock the institution up, we cage the Spirit. But if we destroy the institution that bears the Tradition, where will the Spirit go? All of the innovations that last are Spirit-driven. The rest pass like so much straw in the wind. Organized religion may be down, but it is not out. There remains a necessity to balance form and Spirit.

Moving Forward With Grace, One Step at a Time

I like to watch the children at our church as they work on new behaviors. It is a joy to behold little Annie pull herself up to stand, when only a few weeks ago this was an impossible task. Watching babies take their first steps is also amusing. Georg Konrad, a Hungarian writer, wrote his memories of learning to walk. He said it was like falling, only just as you thought you would fall over, you put forward a foot and stopped yourself. And you would continue, teetering and almost falling, but yet moving forward. Walking. What a triumph!

Spiritual growth is made up of small victories like this. We do not wake up one day thoroughly changed from what we were yesterday; small changes enable us to improve over time. In the end, the result may look like massive change from where we began, but on a day-to-day basis we fight the demons and, once in awhile, overcome one, by baby steps.

We would like our lives to be transformed from selfishness to selflessness, even as a child wants to move from standstill to walking. But changes happen by increments, not all at once. We make a decision to act differently in one instance and thus we alter our behavior toward what we believe is better. So, for instance, instead of engaging in road rage when somebody cuts us off, we make a conscious decision not to respond by word or gesture. We reach inward and deny our selfish ego the pleasure of feeling smug against the offending driver, and we simply let the incident go. As a result, we feel better about ourselves and we decide to try that behavior again.

Notice, therefore, that spiritual growth is not distant or mysterious or separated from the everyday. The transformation occurs within mundane situations. As we seek spiritual growth, we become different because we develop insight to avoid the traps and pitfalls that lie in wait, the everyday temptations that are so difficult to bypass.

Spiritual growth is not some other, better, or bigger life that awaits us on the far side of the one we live from day to day. Instead, it *is* that daily life, transformed. We pray "give us this day our daily bread" to remind ourselves, first of all, that each day's bread is a gift from God and, secondly, that our daily bread is precisely where we receive God. This is nothing extraordinary.

The Old Testament prophets were not interested in exploring mystical realms beyond the ordinary stuff of living day-to-day. Their understanding and proclamation of God is down-to-earth. They call us, again and again, to tasks small and great that enable righteousness to "flow like water."

Of all the religions of the ancient near East, the Hebrew religion tied people to compassion and mercy, values of *this* world. Rabbi Abraham Joshua Heschel wrote that, for the prophets, the greatest sin is not our failure to perform religious rites; rather, it is our callousness toward our fellows. To know God we are not required to scale the heights of mystic splendor; we are "to do justice, love kindness, and walk humbly with your God" (Micah 6:8). And this we can only do one small baby step at a time, because it takes so long to root out self-centeredness.

St Mark the Monk, who lived in Egypt in the fifth century, wrote that three "giants" block our spiritual path: forgetfulness, laziness, and ignorance. These enemies lock us into our own passions and prohibit us from living toward God and our fellow man. Remembering to respond to situations in small but novel ways can free us from these enemies.

Arrogance: A Block to Spiritual Life

The Desert hermits said: "If you see a young person climbing up to heaven by his own strength, catch him by the foot and drag him back to earth. It is not good for him."

This story does not mean that people can climb to heaven. That misses the point, and besides, it is impossible. But there are those who, in their arrogance, believe that it is possible. But we do not have the strength, and occasionally we need someone to grab our ankles and yank us back to reality.

As far as I know, every spiritual tradition worth its salt eschews arrogance as a means to progress in the life of the Spirit. Arrogance is counter-productive because it pushes us upon our own resources, which quickly run out.

St Anthony of the Desert (251-356) was, and remains, the premier example of the Desert monk; he was the original model. His life story is told in a book written by St Athanasius (296-373), the greatest theologian of the age writing about the greatest monastic of the age. He who poured forth words to explain God to other people wrote about one who poured forth silence to allow God to work in others' lives. The sizeable community that he formed considered St Anthony to be full of the Holy Spirit, yet he never elaborated on his relationship with

God. Fearing that he would be seen as arrogant, he embraced a path of quiet, solitude, silence, and minimal speech as his form of communication.

Another teacher from whom I continue to learn is Tatiana Goricheva, one of the underground Christians in the last period of the Soviet empire who learned about the faith under pressure. She was so taken by the importance of the teachings she heard and learned in that Russian pressure cooker that she said, "Every word must be a sacrifice. Otherwise it is better to keep silent." I remind myself of this, especially in those times when I am tempted to fill the air with chatter.

Contrast the attitudes of St Anthony and Tatiana Goricheva to the arrogance that surrounds us these days. People of all ages rail against beliefs they do not understand. People who are still practically children dismiss traditions that have thousands of years of history behind them, as if none of this mattered, as if whole cultures were not built upon the lessons of those historical beliefs. If we cannot get it in a sound byte, they think, it is not worth listening any further. And all of this arrogance is matched by an equal amount of ignorance.

I refer not only to arrogance toward Christianity. Other traditions do not fare well, either. Many people who explore Buddhism want a pop version; they are unwilling to probe the depths of the tradition, and they do not wish to understand the Buddha's historical context. Years ago, Alan Watts, that great "religious entertainer," as he called himself, wrote the trenchant pamphlet *Beat Zen, Square Zen and Zen*, in which he gently called those who wanted cheap Buddhism to drop the illusion that they could get it wholesale. Nothing worth having comes without expense or hard work. This is at least as true in spiritual matters as it is in economics.

Arrogance is a form of seduction that entices us to rely on our ego. This move ironically takes us farther from the very truth we seek. Verse 26 of the *Tao Te Ching* says, "The wise cultivate inner strength and tranquility. That is why they are not seduced by addictive temptations." Tranquility leads us past the temptation to arrogance and entices us to enter the spiritual traditions.

Precepts on the Pathway to Spiritual Life

Abandon all preconceived content to the word "God."

God is never a past experience, but always a present reality. God may be better described in terms of a verb rather than a noun, as if to say that God is ongoing, and not a static concept.

Acknowledge that all religious discourse or description is ultimately inadequate. Just as you cannot understand a butterfly by killing it and tacking it to a board, so you cannot ultimately understand God by studying about God. Words serve only as guides to the experience of the Divine.

Begin with intellectual assent to the Faith. Seek out the best spiritual doctors of past and present within the faith. Avoid charlatans.

Withdraw into pregnant silence; do not speak, but listen. Above all do not expect miracles. In fact, do not expect anything.

Become aware of the ways you justify your hang-ups by incorporating them into a religion. This includes gender, race, fear, and insecurity, among others. Ask that demons be exorcised.

Ignore the external differences by which people separate themselves one from another, such as age, gender, race, creed, or status.

Know that belief and faith are not the same thing. Belief is an accumulation of data that gives a static equation of support or credibility in something or someone. Faith is a process of relationship with reality and is thus dynamic and moving.

Realize that any religious experience that separates you from others and leads you to judge them as inferior is false.

Understand that any religious experience that changes you into someone you are not is false. Authentic religious experience changes you on a deeper level to become the person you already are. Transformations move toward the fullness of humanity, not away from it.

Do not get hung up over forms and methods used to seek a contemplative mood. Form is of no importance in relation to content and is, at best, a vehicle. Do not confuse form with content.

Do not worry that those who profess no belief in God use religious techniques for self-help. Many people use meditation forms because they are beneficial to their lives. There are a variety of techniques on the behavioral level that enable people to become freer without considering any content.

Utilize the best of the Tradition. This includes people-resources and spiritual directors. There are people who know how to help you move, though this is uncommon to western mentality and especially to the almost irrational individualism of the American consciousness. Guidance can help you avoid pitfalls and blind alleys.

Do not go it alone. The liturgical life of the church is not a substitute for contemplation and prayer; it is the deepest corporate form of prayer and acts simultaneously as a check and balance for your individual perceptions.

Be careful of artificial inducements lest you be duped into thinking or believing you cannot get to the level of perception they provoke or provide without them. Prayer and meditation are not escapes from life but aids to enter more deeply into its flow, and hence into the flow of one's own true life.

Avoid false conceptions of prayer, especially those that suggest that prayer is telling God about something God does not already know, or begging for things inconsistent with the true growth of the self.

Undue emphasis on survival needs, creature comfort, or material security bar us from the path. Take a look at your real needs; they are different from your wants, most of which are culturally conditioned.

Go beyond appearance to reality. Things are not what they seem. Seeing is only vision when it touches the level of reality, and God is always below the level of social constructions we call "reality." "All religion is but a looking," said Simone Weil, and that is what we seek – vision into the nature of reality.

God works within the material realm; there is no "higher level" to move to. There is only depth where once there was superficiality.

Balancing Between the Wind and the Markers

Pentecost is the festival of the donation of the Holy Spirit to the church. We believe that the Spirit of God was there from the beginning, of course, "hovering" over the waters of creation as it says in the Book of Genesis, but we celebrate Pentecost as the birthday of the church. According to the Acts of the Apostles, the Spirit called a crowd of people – all of whom spoke different languages – into a new fellowship following the preaching of Peter the Apostle.

The symbolism here is clear: in the Book of Genesis a confusion of tongues (the Tower of Babel) renders people unable to understand one another across tribal and linguistic lines. Communication has been broken, a sad and sorry fact that continues to haunt humanity to this day. Pentecost symbolizes a reversal of this inability, offering the hope of a pathway and a potential community in which people not only dream of, but also experience, a common language that binds them together.

We Christians inherited the festival of Pentecost, like so much in our faith and life, from our Jewish background. Pentecost was and still is called *Shavuot*, which means "weeks," and refers to the fact that the festival occurs seven weeks after Passover. Pentecost is "fifty" in Greek, and bears the same idea as the Hebrew.

In the Orthodox Church we have welcomed people who come from a Pentecostal background, a specific approach to Christianity that focuses on the Holy Spirit's presence in the church. They have told me that they did not know any other churches that emphasized the Spirit so much – until they came into Orthodoxy, where the Spirit is everywhere. In fact, we begin each service with a prayer invoking the Presence of the Spirit:

O Heavenly King, the Comforter, the Spirit
    of Truth,
Who art everywhere present and fillest all things:
Treasury of Blessings and Giver of Life,
Come and abide in us and save our souls, O
    Good One.

John's Gospel emphasizes that the Spirit leads us into all the truth. This has sometimes been forgotten or overlooked when institutions and leaders take the reins too tightly and forbid the Holy Spirit's freedom. Sometimes, it seems, the dove of the Spirit has been strangled and all its feathers plucked.

Among the Jews, Pentecost, or *Shavuot*, is the festival that commemorates the giving of Torah, those instructions for life that come from God, according to the tradition. In the book of Deuteronomy, the "second giving of the Law," God says, "I set before you death and life. Therefore choose life." *L'chaim!* To Life!

Sometimes we in the church have strangled the Spirit in our rush to codify and classify beliefs and actions. We walk a delicate and fragile balance between hearing, receiving, and studying the Word, and allowing the Spirit to blow free as the wind – which is what the word Spirit means, in both Greek and Hebrew. Jesus himself notes the freedom of the Spirit in the Gospel of John.

This form of religion was not intended as a boundary marking community off from community, but as a cohesive force to bring disparate communities together as one. The sad truth is that we – and I speak here primarily of Christian communities – have so often erected, rather than torn down, barriers between us, not to mention boundaries between us and other religious expressions. It is not easy to follow the wind of the Spirit; in fact it is serious and hard work. But we are called to a lifelong pursuit of those attitudes, goals, and values that can unify the human family.

6

SAINT AIDAN

AUGUST 31

CHAPTER 6

Supplication

ST AIDAN

St Aidan was an Irish monk who studied under St Senan on Scattery Island, an island in the Shannon Estuary off the coast of Kilrush, County Clare. He became a monk of Iona, where St Columba established his monastery. He was eventually made the first bishop and abbot of Lindisfarne, the well-known small island off the coast of Northeastern England. Lindisfarne continues to serve the church and receive pilgrims to this day.

During his lifetime, St Aidan was called upon to do many important tasks for the church. King Oswald of Northumbria, the region in the northeast of England by the Scottish border, became a great friend and supporter of his, having met Aidan when he was studying in Ireland. King Oswald enlisted Aidan to help convert his pagan subjects, and continued to do much for Aidan and the Irish missionaries until the king's death in battle at Maserfield near Oswestry, August 5, 642.

Because he was so even-tempered, Aidan was chosen to replace the original missioner to the Anglo-Saxons, who had proven too hotheaded for the job. Aidan arrived in Northumbria in 635 and established his headquarters at Lindisfarne, a tidal island. At low tide it can be reached by walking across the sand to it, but at high tide it is separated from the mainland. It proved to be a great center from which prayer and mission radiated to other parts of the North. Aidan's commission was successful; his mission efforts proved to be crucial in the conversion of the Anglo-Saxons who populated the region.

Among Aidan's many Anglo-Saxon proteges were St Hilda of Whitby and St Cuthbert, both of whom we include in our list of examples of Celtic virtue.

At Lindisfarne, each of Aidan's monk companions had a soul friend, read the Bible constantly, and learned and prayed the psalms as personal prayers. As he moved out from Lindisfarne, Aidan also founded other mission outposts, including the monastery at Melrose.

St Aidan is known for having walked everywhere, eschewing the privilege of riding horseback so that he could relate directly with everyone he came in contact with. He treated each person he encountered as Christ himself, and held them in a spirit of prayer.

St Aidan taught by example even more than by words. He was noted for his prayer, his work ethic, and his honesty in dealing with others. He did not hesitate to call the rich and mighty on their behavior, and ensured that the poor and needy were brought to the attention of those who had the means to assist them.

Stories of St Aidan attribute to him the most ancient and enduring trait of true Christian spirituality: care and love for the poor and the stranger. At the same time, he insisted that his followers be people of both action and contemplation. He may well have shared the motto of St Benedict and his monasteries: *Ora et labora*, "work and pray."

The Venerable Bede, Aidan's biographer and historian of the early English church, wrote more affectionately of Aidan than he did of any other saint. The same qualities that appealed to Bede were responsible for St Aidan's appeal as a teacher and pastor – a passionate love of goodness tempered with warmth, humility, and gentleness. Bede wrote that, "He was a pontiff inspired with a passionate love of virtue, but at the same time full of a surpassing mildness and gentleness."

St Aidan died at Bamburgh on the last day of August, 651, and his remains were carried to Lindisfarne. His feast day is August 31.

TROPAR

> *O holy Bishop Aidan,*
> *Apostle of the North and light of the*
> *Celtic Church,*
> *Glorious in humility, noble in poverty,*
> *Zealous monk and loving missionary,*
> *Intercede for us sinners,*
> *That Christ our God may have mercy on*
> *our souls.*

Listen for the Heartbeat of God

The Psalms are the hymnbook of the Bible, and in due time they became the hymnbook of humanity. St Athanasius (296-373) wrote, "the Psalter is a book that includes the whole life of humanity, all conditions of the mind, and all movements of thought." Joseph Hertz (1872-1946), Chief Rabbi of England, said, "the Psalms translate into simple speech the spiritual passion of the scholar and give utterance, with the beauty born of truth, to the humble longing and petition of the unlettered peasant."

The pattern of the Psalms informs Jewish and Christian prayer and worship, from Protestants to Roman Catholics to Orthodox Christians. But it is among the Celts that we find the most winsome and alluring forms. Celtic prayer is grounded in the melody of the Psalter. That is why triads – as in "Christ above me, Christ below me, Christ within me" from St Patrick's Breastplate – mark the prayers.

A second characteristic of the Psalms is something that scholars call *parallelism*. This is the striking note whereby one verse of a Psalm enhances the preceding one, sometimes by affirmation and sometimes by negation. Here are a few examples from the King James Version:

> "I will bless the Lord at all times; his praise shall
>   continually be in my mouth" (Psalm 34:1).
> "My flesh and my heart faileth; but God is the
>   strength of my heart, and my portion for-
>   ever" (73:26).
> "The heavens declare the glory of God, and the
>   firmament showeth his handiwork" (19:1).

Among the Celtic peoples, especially those of the British Isles, prayer was not so much a formal exercise as it was a habit of the heart. This we all could cultivate to great advantage. On a *60 Minutes* special on the monks of Mt. Athos, the mountain of faith on the coast of Greece, one monk answered a question put by the reporter, "I am praying all the time, even when I am speaking with you or responding to you." The monk was referring to the Jesus Prayer – "Lord Jesus Christ, have mercy on me" – basic to Orthodox Christians. But such immediacy is the soul of all Christian and Jewish prayer, and it surfaces particularly in the Celtic tradition.

In the 19th century, the civil servant Alexander Carmichael travelled through the Outer Hebrides, the land's end of the north, off the coast of Scotland, because he knew that the folk tradition of prayer was dying off. He met with ordinary folk, not necessarily monks or priests or nuns, and caught both the vision and the words that underlay their prayer life.

Carmichael compiled his findings in a volume called *Carmina Gadelica*, "Celtic Songs," still in print and available through online search. The people that Carmichael visited sang their prayers, as did the ancient Israelites who wrote the Psalms. One writer has called this kind of prayer, "the music of what happens." This is intimate prayer, prayer that simply celebrates the events of the day, the movement of the sun and clouds and rain, the tasks called for on farm or workplace. Listen:

May peace be upon each thing my eye takes in,
Upon each thing my mouth takes in,
Upon my body that is of earth,
And upon my soul that comes from on high.

God, bless thou thyself my reaping,
Each ridge, and plain, and field,
Each sickle curved, shapely, hard,
Each ear and handful on the sheaf.

This is prayer as the lilting song of the heart set free for God. Such prayer is as natural as breathing or walking or the rising of the sun. We are not too late for this feast of prayer. We can take it into our own hearts, so long as we are still and "listen for the heartbeat of God" (J. Philip Newell). In the quiet it will come. It will come.

The ABCs of Prayer

When we go on an extended vacation, we have to think carefully about how to pack. Specifically, what is the minimum we need to be both comfortable and prepared? Over the years we have learned to carry as little baggage as necessary -- which, by the way, I hope applies to all of my life.

Let us think about this concept in relation to prayer. What is the minimum that we need to be able to make a discipline for ourselves? This is not about cutting corners; it is about finding the level of comfort and preparation that will enable us to pray on a regular and sustained basis. To that end, here are some thoughts.

Many years ago, when I was in graduate school, I asked a professor of practical theology how he thought one could aid a congregation to grow in the faith. I have never forgotten the answer he gave, in words heavily tinged with his German accent: "Well, first you teach the ABCs and then you go on to teach the ABCs." I got the point: basics remain essential. Keep it simple. We are always beginners.

Let A stand for "abbreviated," to mean a short amount of time. My wife Susan is among the thousands of fans of FlyLady, who has a website dedicated to assisting people to deal with the clutter in their lives. FlyLady's basic rule of de-cluttering is "you can do anything for fifteen minutes." So the point is: keep it short or abbreviated, but keep that prayer time. Take five minutes or ten, but take them.

Let B stand for "basic" or simple, in terms of what you say. Try "Lord Jesus Christ, have mercy on me," and with each repetition add a short intercession like "and remember my mother, _____." It is fine to be basic in the content of your prayer. Most prayer is essentially twofold: intercession and thanksgiving. "Gratitude is the heart of prayer," as Brother David Steindl-Rast wrote in his book of the same name, and it is true. From that heart proceeds our concern for the world, beginning with those around us.

Let C stand for "consistency," meaning a disciplined way. Choose a time to do it, whether in the morning or the afternoon or at evening, but strive for consistency. You might find a time during the day when you are occupied with some other task that does not require all your mental energy and use that for prayer. I cycle almost every day, and often I am a lone rider. Once I get into the rhythm of cycling, I turn to prayer. I am amazed at how much ground I cover in my prayer while covering ground on my bicycle.

Many tasks can become prayer themselves if we devote ourselves fully to them, and enter into them as spiritual disciplines. I always enjoy washing dishes as a form of prayer. Cutting vegetables is another one. Gardening, especially weeding, can be a time for prayer. Susan used the second rinse cycle on our washer, which had to be monitored, as a prayer time.

So here it is: A stands for abbreviated time; it does not have to be long to be heartfelt. B stands for basic words and patterns; do not get flustered trying to say what you want. C stands for consistency, to use the same time or the same activity for your prayer.

Our prayers relate to the corporate prayer of the church, which carries forth, binds together, and offers up all our individual petitions. May our prayer life be blessed.

Praise and Thanksgiving, Father, We Offer

When Thanksgiving rolls around each November, I am particularly reminded of how the Celtic tradition of giving thanks revolves around gratitude and praise in both song and words. The blending of text and tune is notable in so much of the hymnody of Wales and Ireland in particular, though not limited to those areas by any means.

Hear this point, well stated by the Anglo-Welsh poet and artist David Jones: "If poetry is praise, as prayer is, it can never coexist with any malignant and persistent criticism of the nature of things." So when we offer gratitude and praise, the intermediate problems that beset us or others must be laid aside. We are called to offer praise beyond ourselves – and that means to God. Thanksgiving is cut short unless it finds its goal In God. This is why so many events of "thanksgiving" fall short in our age.

The twentieth-century Welsh poet Waldo Williams said that the purpose of praise is to recreate an unblemished world. As the Christian writer, A. M. Allchin, points out, however, this is a problem in our age. We have become accustomed to belittling things, to the art of the put-down, to endless grousing about this, that, and the other thing so that praise and thanksgiving have been lost. For those who grew up in the age of entitlement, it may be difficult ever to achieve anything even remotely like thanks. If we are entitled to everything we get, then why bother to give thanks for anything? After all, we deserved it. It was our right and privilege, and nothing to give thanks for.

One of my favorite poets is Dylan Thomas, a stormy figure who crafted great things with words. Although he was Welsh, he did not know the Welsh language. Yet he was able to bring sound and meaning together in ways that seem peculiar to that tongue. In the introduction to a volume of his collected poems, he says, "These poems, with all their crudities, doubts, and confusions, are written for the love of Man and in praise of God, and I'd be a damn fool if they weren't."

Allchin makes the point that when we demean other things in our life, we really demean ourselves, and when we praise others, we uplift ourselves. The old adage applies, "One is never so tall as when falling on the knees in prayer." This brings us to our final point.

Praise, thanksgiving, and worship go together. The central act of worship in many churches is called *Eucharist,* a Greek word that means "thanksgiving," in which the stuff of this world, transformed through manufacture – handwork – is offered to God in the act of thanks. It is, in the words of the service, "a mercy of peace, a sacrifice of praise." These words are said at the beginning of the great prayer that sets aside the bread and the wine to be body and blood of Christ for the faithful.

In our cynical age we have lost the obvious meaning of this act, which is that the makings of our hands and the matter of nature, when offered up in thanks, are returned to us as signs of the presence of God in our lives. We lose sight of this, particularly when we degenerate into grousing and moaning based on the idea that the universe owes us something. Perhaps this year we may regain this perspective.

Blessings on You, Animals Definitely Included

In January of every year, we hold our annual pet blessing in our little Orthodox mission parish. We have been both surprised and overwhelmed by the response. Last year about seventy dogs showed up, bringing their owners in tow. What is going on here?

Christians have been blessing things forever, maintaining the practice in line with Judaism. Other religions bless animals and material things, as well. In Orthodox prayer books there are blessings for flocks, for herds, for bees. We pray that animals do not experience drought or disease even as we pray for ourselves. Pet owners, regardless of their religion or lack thereof, want the best for their animals, and pet blessings have become a way to express that. This is affirmed on the day of the blessing.

The first reason for our service is to give thanks for Creation and its manifold gifts to us, not least of which are animals for livestock and animals for friends – most notably cats, dogs, and birds. We come together to give glory to God for the magnificence of creation. As the old British hymn goes, "All things bright and beautiful, all creatures great and small, all things wise and wonderful, the Lord God made them all," which served as title for that lovely series of books by the veterinarian whose pen name was James Herriot.

Jews and Christians take seriously the biblical mandate to master creation. We regard ourselves as husbandmen or stewards – a word, incidentally, from old English that originally meant "the keeper of a sty." At our best, we are tenders and managers; at our worst, we are menaces and destroyers. The call to be good stewards is for everyone. We have learned late in our history that it is and must be everyone's concern.

A second reason we bless our animals is to remind ourselves that they deserve mercy and love from us, and not miserable or abusive treatment. This does not mean that we value them above other people, but that we value them in their own right as animate creatures that share sensibility with us. In our community of faith, we echo the Buddhist who vows to "save all sentient beings." The rise in consultation with veterinarians about our pets, let alone our livestock, indicates that the majority of people are willing to put into practice their goodwill to animals.

Third, we pray for animals as we would pray for members of our family or friends, or even our enemies, for that matter. We want our animals to enjoy good health and long life within the constraints of their animal natures. One of our great Orthodox thinkers, St Maximos the Confessor, put this way: "Man is not a being isolated from the rest of creation; by nature man is bound up with the whole of the universe … On his way to union with God, man does not leave creatures behind, but gathers in his love the whole cosmos disordered by sin, that it may be transfigured by grace."

Animals are not rocks or rivers. They are "animated beings," which means they have a soul. Their soul is not a human soul, it is an animal soul, but we Orthodox Christians at least affirm that they have souls. They share in the glory of God. They are more than companions; they are a sign of the power and beauty of the created order. They connect us to wildness since, even when domesticated, they remain a "breed apart" with feral instincts and habits.

A final reason for this tradition – may our blessing of animals remind us to bless our human families and friends.

Can These Bones Live? Experiencing Faith

I have heard people acknowledge that spiritual experiences are wonderful and, for that matter, undeniably real. But they also say that the rituals of worship that grow from these experiences are man-made, and thus dispensable.

We may disbelieve the Biblical account of Moses receiving the Ten Words on Mount Sinai, for example, but we cannot deny the impact of their reception on the construction of the Jewish faith. We may deny the resurrection of Jesus, but we are surely unable to deny the growth of the church as a result of belief in this Resurrection. The Hebrew slaves of Egypt, who least expected to be rescued, found themselves free, if wandering in the desert. The disciples of Jesus, who least expected him to be raised from death, experienced him alive and personally drawing them onward in mission.

Experiences of wonder and awe do not automatically lead to worship, but it is equally true that without such profound experiences worship cannot arise.

We try to tame our experiences of wonder and corral them into a narrow frame of interpretation. Yes, there are aspects that yield to sociological, anthropological, or psychological explanation, but such categories neither contain them nor fully explain them. Every interpretation misses some aspects because the experiences are like facets of a diamond which, when turned, reveals new light and another brilliance. The problem of trying to communicate such experiences shows that they are mysteries.

We can talk about mysteries, but talking never exhausts their meaning. Mystery names an experience that can be expressed but not comprehended. Times of awe lead directly to worship and adoration. Moses stands before the bush that burns but is not consumed, and he is awestruck.

Awe is not a feeling. It is a clear mental and even physical sensation in the presence of mystery. In the fourth century, teachers of the church called the process of becoming a Christian through the rituals of baptism, anointing, and first communion at Pascha (Easter), "the awe-inspiring rites of initiation."

Certainly the ritual constructions of religion are man-made – who else would make them? – but are they dispensable? We use rituals we do not often acknowledge as such – handshakes, putting hand over heart at the national anthem, opening doors for others, kissing on the cheek, family gatherings at funerals and weddings. Ritual is protocol to get us past awkward moments. Religion is grounded in ritual, too, but it is more than protocol.

The religious use of rituals intends to communicate the mystery they are based on. Through them, we who live today participate in the *reality* of those events that shaped the faith and, ultimately, the practices of a particular faith-tradition. The Seder enables Jews to experience the first Passover at Passover of this year; Pascha enables Christians to experience the resurrection of Christ in their own bodies and hearts in this year.

We are not out of the woods yet, however. If ritual arises to communicate mystery, how can it do so if mystery is essentially incommunicable? That is why we amplify or circumvent the words through symbol, song, and story; we call for pageant and physical participation. We remember the event in our bodies.

This is not memory as recall of facts locked in the past. "To remember" in the biblical sense means that a past event becomes present, *with the fullness of its meaning*, to our experience. Like the Exodus, the festival of freedom. Like the Eucharist, the feast of faith. These events surround our present moment and bring us renewed life. For that we need ritual; and faith traditions are borne by ritual.

A Short Introduction to the Jesus Prayer

The Jesus prayer is simple, and straight out of the Gospels: "Lord Jesus Christ, have mercy on me." As Jesus walked by, people used these words to implore him to attend to their needs. And so it came down through history to us. Sometimes the prayer is embellished: "Lord Jesus Christ, Son of God, have mercy on me a sinner."

The idea is to say it slowly and meditatively, as you would a prayer. It may help to regulate your breathing to the words, but this has not been deemed necessary. In fact, Theophan the Recluse (19th century Russian bishop) says that too much attention to the technique and method of using the prayer is "spiritual hedonism." The point is to be in the presence of Christ, not to fool with techniques or gimmicks.

It is natural to start praying with the *oral* stage; we recite the words in intercession, petition, thanksgiving, or supplication. Then we move to the *mental* stage, and we begin to pray with a focused mind. Finally comes the prayer of our *heart*, when we pray in silence because we are enfolded in the heart of God. When we reach this stage, there is nothing but rejoicing in the Presence of God who knows all our needs and cares.

Through the Jesus prayer we draw near to God, who has already drawn near to us in Christ and through the Spirit, but whose Presence we are tempted to forget – especially in times of trial and tribulation. Contrary to popular thought, God is more forgotten in those times than when we are feeling blessed in life.

The Jesus prayer assists us in two ways. First, it is a genuine act of *worship*, like other forms of prayer or hymnody. Secondly, it helps move us toward deeper prayer by giving us a *discipline*, which grows on us the longer we practice it.

The discipline of the Jesus Prayer can be assisted by the use of the prayer rope (called a *chotki* in Slavic and a *kombouskini* in Greek). St Pachomius, a monastic abbot, invented the rope in the fourth century, though the prayer goes back to the earliest church. This type of prayer rope typically has 33, 50, or 100 knots, with a wooden bead separating each ten knots. The bead acts as a reminder to focus our hearts and minds if they have strayed. The rope has a knotted cross with or without a tassel on the circle. We hold the rope in our left hand and run through the knots one by one using our thumb and forefinger. It is customary to begin by holding the cross and saying "In the Name of the Father and of the Son and of the Holy Spirit. Amen."

We may also use the Jesus prayer to intercede for others. We simply include them either aloud or silently on one or more of the knots: "Lord Jesus Christ, have mercy on...." The point is not to get stuck on the mechanism, but to use it simply as an aid for our prayer. If the rope takes up too much of our attention, we have lost the idea and need to go back and begin again.

Do not overdo the discipline; begin by daily using the short rope three times with one prayer on each knot and expand from there, slowly. I advise you to seek out a spiritual father or mother to aid you in your developing prayer life.

Begin Within to Move Out to Healing

As believers in Christ, we can avail ourselves of a history, a rich and full corporate life that, for the Orthodox Church, stretches over two thousand years. I was reminded of this again, as often happens, in an alternative setting. We went to Vespers – the evening service of prayer and praise and psalms – at the church we attend when on vacation in California. As I stood there listening to the choir sing the familiar psalms of the Vesper service, my fingers traced the words of our simplest yet most profound prayer, *kyrie eleison* – in English "Lord have mercy." As I traced my prayers on the intricate knots that make up the wrist bracelet we call a *chotki*, breathing in and breathing out rhythmically, I commemorated everyone in our congregation and in my circle of acquaintances in the Mesilla Valley, and all of the departed whom I uphold in my prayers.

Tears welled in my eyes at the serenity and completeness of it all. Here I am, I thought, definitely a 21st century man, immersed in this age-old history that embraces people of all times, cultures and conditions. On the walls of the church are icons of American saints – Herman of Alaska, Innocent of Alaska who later became the Metropolitan of Moscow, and John of San Francisco. Over there is Elizabeth the New Martyr, and here is Nina the Illuminator of Georgia, a woman who in her youth (in the fourth century) worked to convert an entire country. And I am also commemorating the saints in the Mesilla Valley, the ones who are so intimately tied to my heart and our community in Christ.

That experience got me to thinking about the heart of it all. All people, not just the devout, have reason to live ethically, to strive for justice and mercy on all levels of society, to care for the homeless, and to soften the heartless. But when there is no core to our caring, no heart beneath our cordiality, no peace at our center, then we may find ourselves running around doing good simply to make ourselves feel better, or superior to those "less fortunate." My favorite saint, Seraphim of Sarov, said it best: "Acquire peace in the Holy Spirit and thousands around you will be saved."

Frenetic activity will not save the world. During the height of the Vietnam conflict, Thomas Merton, a Roman Catholic monk, reminded folks that the task of the monk is to uphold the world through prayer. In Holy Orthodoxy, we consider this the task of every Christian, for whom our monks and nuns lead the way by their commitment and their intensity.

Although we are as distracted and distorted by our culture as anyone, we can learn our limits and boundaries. We can bind up what wounds we can, both our own and those of other people. We can try not to inflict any further wounds on a hurt and vulnerable world. But above all, the true way to find healing and wholeness is to go inward, by descending through prayer and contemplation, and to bring the conditions and circumstances of the world before the fragile Presence. To fight for wholeness.

All of this is why we must stay focused on prayer and worship, following the pattern of the church throughout its history. It is easy to get lost and stray from that healing Presence. That is why we return again and again to that Presence – in silence, in speech, in song, in symbol, and in sacrament. It is the only way we know.

A Longing for the Unattainable Future

The Welsh language has one of those wonderful words we sometimes stumble across that seem untranslatable because of their depth and breadth of meaning. The word is *hiraeth*, pronounced here-eyeth. If you look in your nearby Welsh dictionary, it will tell you the word means "longing, nostalgia." No other language has a word quite like it, for *hiraeth* seems to be a deeply Welsh emotion. It is a combination of two words that together mean, literally, long field. Imagine we are on the prairies of Kansas or Saskatchewan, where the fields stretch forever, making it hard to cross to what we want on the other side. That is the inner feeling of *hiraeth*. *Hiraeth* is longing for an unattainable end. The horizon keeps receding as we think we are getting close.

Hiraeth is more than just longing, however: friend Robert Jones says "It's a combination of longing, nostalgia, almost an obsession for a thing, a place, a person or state of being that you may have had in the past or dream about having in the future. You cannot have it, at least not right now, and you may never have it or attain it." Welsh people have felt *hiraeth* when they migrate to other places, but of course one can feel it at home in Wales as well. Maybe it is a peculiarly Celtic quality of soul. I have been among Irish folks who show a similar feeling. That feeling resonates through Celtic music with its haunting, plaintive melodies, often in minor key.

Perhaps other languages cannot match the precise term, but I am sure that we have all known the experience and the feeling at some time in our lives. John Mayall, the British Blues king, has a great song called "Blues for the Lost Days," that captures some of the feeling. Those days, he sings, "are gone but still live in the heart. There won't be a counterpart." That is the backward look of *hiraeth*, the nostalgia part.

We long for many things: lost times, as John Mayall sang, particularly the scent of people whom we have lost through death or distance. Lost opportunities, paths not taken when the wood opened onto a fork in the road and we took one rather than the other. Lost vistas, places that we remember from earlier times that seemed so simple, when now we are overwhelmed by complexity. Will we recapture those vistas, opportunities, or lost friends and family in some future? That is the longing of *hiraeth*.

There is a forward-looking aspect to *hiraeth*, however, that is even more important. It is the sense that we have a goal or end in life, but it always seems to be out of reach, just like that receding horizon line. We can translate this from Wales onto the universe because *hiraeth* cannot, should not, in the end be confined to one place.

Some folks say that this longing is the mainspring for religion: we cannot recover the past or attain a future, so we take refuge in religion. On the other hand are those who say that the sense of the eternal, so vivid that we can almost taste it, inspires hope for the unattainable that will, in time, become realized. I side with the latter.

The letter to the Hebrews in the New Testament says, "Faith is the substance of things hoped for." It is almost tangible; that is what substance means. We remember the future in hope. And that, my friends, is what *hiraeth* is about: it is a longing unsullied by the vagaries of time or the chasms of distance. It is an affliction of the heart that draws us inevitably toward a future we see but cannot touch, a future full of peace and compassion. It is the allure of the divine, beckoning us toward fulfillment.

SAINT BRIGID

FEBRUARY 1

CHAPTER 7

Spiritual Friendship

ST BRIGID

Shrouded in the mists of history and the Emerald Isle itself, St Brigid is sometimes thought to be a specter made up of early goddess legends, imposed on a Christian landscape. Indeed there is a goddess Brigid of fire, light, and healing in the background of Irish folk legend and religion. And she and St Brigid exhibited similar attributes. But most of Christianity teaches that the person who attained unto sainthood was quite definitely alive, and very much her own woman.

Generations of Irish Christians and many others love St Brigid deeply. Known as St Ffraid in Wales, she is equally honored there. And as "Mary of the Gaels" she was considered patroness of pilgrims throughout the British Isles until well into the Middle Ages.

Tradition tells us that St Brigid's dates are 452-524, and her accomplishments were many. She founded a monastery at Kildare that lasted for centuries, eventually becoming one of the three most important monastic centers of Ireland. The name Kildare means "the church of the oak," referring to the spot on which she was commissioned to found the community. She is also reputed to have been one terrific brewmaster, having served up goodly amounts of her beer there.

St Brigid's annual commemoration overlaps with the Festival of the Presentation (which is still called Candlemas in many churches for the blessing of fire on that day), in remembrance of the everlasting flame at Kildare that, according to historians, was kept burning from the fifth century until the 1200s.

Above all, St Brigid is remembered as a great soul friend to both students and pilgrims alike. Her famous quote, "anyone without a soul friend is like a body without a head," is repeated often. Brigid seems to have had an inclusive spirit, drawing people both into her confidence and her community. In that spirit she engaged in spiritual counsel with many who came to her, high and low, Christian or no.

Unlike many of the women saints whose lives are associated with suffering, pain, and great difficulties establishing themselves in their roles within the church, St Brigid was readily accepted as a leader. She was seen early on as a director of souls, and her ministry was not only unchallenged, but lauded. This was demonstrated in many ways, among them the relationships she had with others whom we now regard as saints: Brendan the Voyager of Clonfert, Finnian of Clonard, and Kevin of Glendalough, men whose influence would in turn inspire the creation of new monasteries.

Thinking of St Brigid, I cannot help but compare her to a modern saint, Maria Skobtsova, who was only recently canonized by the Russian church and received by others. Maria Skobtsova was an unusual candidate for sanctity because she did not follow the usual monastic path of silence and withdrawal from the world. Instead, she put herself forward during World War II as an advocate for the poor, and especially for Jews. She eventually paid for this with her life. But unto the end she remained a strong, fiercely independent woman, though tonsured as a nun and thus under discipline. St Brigid reminds me of St Maria Skobtsova in so many ways, but particularly because of her independence and her ability to console and counsel people from many walks of life.

St Brigid's legacy towers over Irish Christianity, a model for those of us who would counsel others both inside and outside the faith. She shows us how to gently lead people forward into a new or renewed faith posture that expands beyond the limitations of every institution, while remaining true to the institution's burning heart. Her feast day is February 1.

TROPAR

> *O holy Brigid, you became sublime through*
> *your humility,*
> *And flew on the wings of your longing for God.*
> *When you arrived in the eternal City and*
> *appeared before your Divine Spouse,*
> *Wearing the crown of virginity,*
> *You kept your promise to remember those who*
> *have recourse to you.*

You shower grace upon the world,
And multiply miracles.
Intercede with Christ our God that He may save
our souls.

Seeing Our Churches as Therapeutic Centers

In the Book of Acts in the New Testament, we see the early church at work doing the same ministry of healing that we find in the ministry of Jesus. These healing stories are meant to demonstrate the continuity of faith and life, particularly in regard to the healing power the church brings to the world.

When reading these stories, we are tempted to console ourselves, saying that this was the early church, a much different period in history than now. This becomes a way to excuse ourselves when we see the woeful lack of healing in so many churches, perhaps even our own. Often our churches look moribund, destitute and struggling, rather than full of liveliness, healing, and hope. It is easy to lose sight of purpose, calling, and ministry in the welter of activity, administration, and distractions of modern life.

Every story of healing in the New Testament comes to us with a message on two levels, one physical and the other spiritual. They are connected; there is a peculiar form of paralysis that is spiritual, and the healing of physical impairment takes that into consideration.

The paralytic is a person who cannot move. Mobility is a major part of our lives. Every physical therapist or trainer will tell us that, as we age, it is particularly important to keep moving and flexible. When our bodies no longer move, when breath no longer moves through them, we are dead.

Any inability to move affects both body and soul. Without mobility we are trapped. We can become inflexible in spirit as well as in body. All this and more is what we are freed from when we gain healing. We are free to move forward once again in our human pilgrimage.

Current psychological researchers like Zachary Beckstead and Ravi Chandra accept that we were meant to be "on pilgrimage," and that our humanity does not require a settled life for completion and fulfillment. This explains the New Testament's emphasis on healing paralytics.

The church is a place of healing, a "hospital for sick souls." In fact, that is its primary characteristic, according to the many explorations of Metropolitan Hierotheos Vlachos, a Greek theologian. The church is meant to be a therapeutic community. If it is not, it is missing the high calling to which it has been called.

The healings that take place today may not seem as dramatic as the ones depicted in scripture, but they are nonetheless real. When people are enabled to drop the crutch of addiction through the power of faith, real healing has happened. When we are enabled to drop the withering limitations of our anger, real healing has happened. When we are enabled to move beyond coldness and disinterest in others, our paralysis has been healed. When we can move beyond the view that sex is the be-all and end-all of life, real healing has occurred.

Unlike so many of the healings recorded in the New Testament, our healings may not be immediate and total. We may need to revisit our pockets of paralysis time and again before they are fully cured. In some churches, the rites of confession and anointing help us to drive out the passions that fuel our particular and personal forms of paralysis. But be assured that those passions *will* yield in the end, and we shall be healed.

St Irenaeus already understood this in the second century when he well said: "The glory of God is a human being fully realized." That realization takes place as we are healed, whether slowly or swiftly, through the power of God.

God Comes Among Us for Healing

I have never been much of a one for religion. That may sound crazy because I am a priest of the Orthodox Church, and therefore deeply involved in religious activities such as leading worship. But hold on a minute and let me explain.

In the theology schools where I trained, we were taught to look carefully at our faith, and at other forms of religion, to see if there was a difference between them. Nobody pushed us to conclusions, as I recall, but it became somewhat obvious that there was one central difference between the way of following Christ and other pathways.

In the other pathways we explored, people were searching for God. The primary movement was, so to speak, from this world to the next. In Christianity and its sister faith Judaism, however, God searches for people. In fact, that is the theme of one of my favorite books out of the Jewish world, *God in Search of Man* by the great rabbi Abraham Joshua Heschel. One old story says that God gets up in the morning, hides in the creation, and then waits in hope that people will find him. But even if they do not, God takes the first step and comes to them.

A lot of people, even if they do not know it or cannot put

it into words, search for God in a difficult and perplexing time. But this searching can become endless. It is possible to remain a seeker all of one's life and never come to a resting place, to get lost in the search itself.

Christians hold, however, that God took the ultimate step of entering the human predicament lock, stock, and barrel. God took the initiative. God came from another realm into this one to announce that he was going to gather us all up in his arms again – and then did it through a cross and by rising to new life.

Our human condition, blemishes and beauty marks alike, was taken up into God because God came among us as a human being. That is the core of Christian faith. St Cyril of Alexandria put it this way: everything that we are has to be brought back into communion with God, or else none of it is. You cannot leave out stuff, particularly not the "bad" stuff.

I have known quite a few people, in fact, who left churches because they could not or did not feel that they were accepted. They hid from other people because they thought – rightly or wrongly – that the others would not accept them for who they were. So they hid their indiscretions, their divorces, their bad relationships with children, their addictions. Apparently they thought that they would not be accepted if they admitted to – what? – being fully human. But you cannot be healed if you are not willing to have God reach into every corner of your life and bring wholeness once again.

All of us are separated and alienated from God, from others, from our deepest selves. Christ came to restore our deep selves and to bring us back into communion with others. He does this precisely by once again opening our clogged relationship with God. If our church does not communicate this properly, then we have fallen into the trap of religion, which is to keep people reaching beyond this world for some imagined fulfillment, rather than allowing God to heal us here and now.

You Just Call Out My Name

Everyone of a certain age remembers Carole King's classic song from her 1971 *Tapestry* album, "You've Got a Friend," with its great lyric. James Taylor made it hugely popular. I am sure that there were churches that used it as a hymn in those experimental worship days. It still speaks to us of a deep need.

Everyone needs friendship. It is the stuff of life, even as bread is the staff of life. And yet friendship was not recognized as a virtue throughout the Christian world until rather late.

The first treatise ever written on friendship came from Aelred (1110-1167), Abbot of Rievaulx Monastery. Despite its French name, Rievaulx is a town near Helmsley in Yorkshire, England. Aelred had so few sources to turn to in the tradition of the church that he had to reach back to Cicero (106-43 BC), the great Roman orator and philosopher, for a template for his book. Cicero had written to his friend Laelius in 44 BC with a treatise he called simply "On Friendship." Aelred used many of Cicero's concepts and issued his book under the title *On Spiritual Friendship*. It is still in print.

Aelred influenced Bernard of Clairvaux, the first person in the Western church to tackle the concept of love on the ground, rather than love for God, since the days when Augustine had written about it centuries earlier. So Aelred's book got some traction in those days.

But despite the attention Aelred's book did get, the issue I have wrestled with is this: Why didn't the church affirm ordinary friendship as a spiritual pathway for so many centuries? A millennium went by before Aelred put quill to parchment and penned his little, and singular, classic – and it was dependent on a Roman model from a millennium before. I think there are two reasons.

First, the church was hesitant to condone much at all in the way of relationships outside of marriage. Monks and nuns were to be celibate, which seems to have meant sexless, or at the very least a personal abandonment of sexuality. It is less than a century until the IV Lateran Council of 1215 (held at Rome) made celibacy mandatory for the priesthood throughout the Western church (Eastern Orthodoxy never adopted this rule). Friendships across sexual lines were frowned upon, despite the fact that some Celtic monasteries had both men's and women's houses. And of course there was the constant worry that friendships between people of the same sex might lead further.

We find the second impediment to the church's affirmation of friendships embedded within the monastic concept of commonality. If, as a monk, you hold all things in common, this idea extends to include your fellow monastics. If one friend becomes more special than another in your world, your favoritism violates the commonality directive.

Time moves on, however, and with its passage the whole concept and reality of friendship was rethought. Today we affirm friendship as a spiritual value and quality in human relationships. As the church recovered its understanding of the ministry of the laity, in the sense that all Christians are called to a life of love and service, friendship began to feel more like a natural part of spirituality.

In today's society, in which so many people are "churchless Christians," it makes sense to affirm natural aspects of living that carry a spiritual quality. Friendship may top this list.

We do not need a whole lot of friends. In fact, it is quite difficult to craft a bevy of friendships. It requires commitment, a certain ruthless honesty, and years of fermentation to come to fruition. I have a handful of friends; some I have had for as long as fifty years, some only a few. I find the variety to be good. As for the rest of the people in my life, I am friendly with them all, but they are really better called acquaintances than friends.

In the early English language we usually call Anglo-Saxon, friendship has a double meaning: that we guarantee the freedom of another, and that we love the person. A friend is someone who loves us enough to allow us to be free. Would to God that we cultivate such friends; they are a blessing.

What's Talk Got to Do With It? Everything.

Years ago, I invested a lot of time and energy into learning about communication. Those lessons have served me in various human relations, and I notice that they keep showing up in different forms. An example is the spate of books by Don Miguel Ruiz, chief of which is called *The Four Agreements*.

It is a simple model of human interaction with four easily remembered points: don't take anything personally, be true to your word, don't make assumptions, and always do the best you can.

So there you have it. The problem, of course, is actually living by the four agreements. Most of us don't. And because we don't, we get into trouble through our deceptions, assumptions, and laziness.

We live by sound bites today. So communication is crippled as we experience instant polarization on the basis of minimal information. For a long time, Twitter messages were limited to 140 characters. Characters, not necessarily even words. Emails can land us in a heap of trouble because they often sound more venomous than we intended. People's reputations can be literally ruined in seconds by anonymous, unsubstantiated rumors. It is a jungle out there in the cyberworld, which is fast becoming the real world.

I believe that God shows up in human dress. By that I mean in all matters and manners human. That is why communication is one of the central tasks we have to master. The Gospel of John opens with the words, "In the beginning was the Word and the Word was with God." Stop right there. Here are grounds enough for contemplating the close connection between good, which is to say truthful, communication and God.

The late Roman Catholic monk Thomas Merton, in his book *New Seeds of Contemplation*, suggested that we are each of us words spoken by God, and we spend our lives learning how to pronounce ourselves. If his metaphor rings at all true, then we had best be sure we are communicating as openly and deeply as we are able.

Communication fails when we reduce another person to a slogan, an image, or a caricature. Lots of that goes on these days, and I suspect that it is one of the main reasons for so much hatred and violence. When we reduce another person to a caricature, we disallow her from stepping forward and presenting herself in a genuine and whole manner. People judge one another on the basis of the scantiest information, which is usually innuendo, and often not even truthful. It is like trying to communicate using only bumper stickers; there is not much mileage in it, but there may be a lot of anger.

Genuine communication involves vulnerability. The Germans call it *Auseinandersetzung*, "putting out and taking in stuff about one another," in my free translation. This would include honest and clear statements of disagreement, without putting the other person down.

Communication is the basis of relationships, so we had better be sure we are doing it right. My brother-in-law, a school administrator, works to improve communication among members of his team. To that end, he has used the book *Fierce Conversations* by Susan Craig Scott. The term "fierce" means robust and untamed. The simplest definition of a fierce conversation is one in which we come out from behind ourselves, into the conversation, and make it real. Scott's theme is that conversations are not about relationships; the conversation is the relationship.

If we couple the idea of fierce conversations with the four agreements, we have gone a long way toward achieving communication without innuendo or put-down. Let us make it a point to seek better communication in our lives. They will be greatly enriched, both mentally and spiritually.

One Significant Conversation

Recently I suggested that people in my circle of acquaintance adopt a practice I try to live by, namely, to have one significant conversation each day with someone they know, and one significant conversation with someone new.

Of course, the latter proves to be much harder to do than the former. But the former is not easy, either. Many people have little or no significant conversation during a day and, furthermore, have gotten used to this as if it were acceptable. Years ago I innocently asked my middle son, who was then living in Boston, if he had one significant conversation each day. He thought I was joking and said it was impossible.

It would be a better world if we all had one significant conversation a day.

What do I mean by a "significant conversation"? First, it does not mean talking about sports, the weather, or your most recent illness, unless it is a spiritual threat to you. Second, it means entering the life of another person and listening as only you can listen to hear the depth in the other. You are uniquely capable of listening to the people in your circle as no one else can. Third, it means interrupting your own schedule to be available for others. I am guessing that one of these three reasons currently stops you from having significant conversations.

When I lived in Chicago, I was teaching among people from many different countries. An African student asked me why Americans say, "How are you?" if they are unwilling to stop and hear the answer. In Africa, he said, people stop and willingly interrupt their own agenda to find out how others really are. The noble art of conversation is not yet dead on African soil.

What does this do for other people? It honors them; it makes them feel as if they are worthwhile, loved, and worthy of our attention. It gives them the option to disclose matters of importance to us, stuff that comes from their depths instead of simply passing off the usual top-of-the-head comments we exchange.

What does this do for us? It makes us keener, sharper, and more attentive to the real person who is before us. We become aware, or we can become aware in a setting of trust, of the full reality of the other person. We have no choice but to become compassionate when we really allow ourselves the gift of conversation.

What does this have to do with God? Plenty. We are made in the image and likeness of God, hence to relate to another human being is to relate to God through the veil of flesh. God shows up in masks, and each one of us is a mask. God made man because he loves stories, says Elie Wiesel; each one of us is a story to be told. So, to use terms I am familiar with, through our listening each of us can be a "little Christ" to another person, as St John Chrysostom said.

The late theological teacher Nelle Morton, in her book *The Journey Is Home*, offers a reversal of our usual metaphors about God. She suggests that, rather than understanding God as Word, we think for a change of God as Hearing. Imagine that: God the great listener, who hears each one of us into speech. The Psalms, for example, are people's attempts to speak to God in all their conditions of life, and God hears. So might we become listeners, for the sake of God's presence in the world, in the lives of those whom we "hear into speech" through conversation.

On Fostering that Significant Conversation

I had the extraordinary fortune to overlap with Henri Nouwen's time at Yale University at the end of the Seventies. Henri was a gregarious Dutch Roman Catholic priest who came to Yale and offered a totally different way of teaching. For example, in his course on spiritual direction he used but one book: the Gospel of Luke. He was the driving force behind interfaith conferences on spirituality. Henri stressed matters of the heart rather than the accumulation of intellectual data. I worked with him in spiritual direction courses, and he encouraged and sponsored me to teach a course on calligraphy and spirituality. I remain grateful for this.

Always a restless spirit, Henri remained at Yale for a decade, with occasional sabbaticals at monasteries like the Abbey of the Genesee, then pushed on to Harvard for a few years, and wound up as pastor to the L'Arche Daybreak community in Toronto – a community of mentally and physically handicapped people. He died, some would say too young, in 1996. His legacy lives on in the many people who read his books or in new readers who discover his lucid style and depth of heart.

I learned, or had confirmed, three important lessons from Henri. First, he believed we have to approach all of life "with open hands" (the title of one of his books). He talked about creating space between people, about allowing others to fill in the space with their own concerns and cares. If only we would not fill in those spaces, he taught, then people would eventually open up and begin to talk about their real concerns, rather than what they present on the surface. Not only their thoughts, but their hearts would become visible, and thus they could approach the spiritual side of their lives in a natural and honest way.

Second, we must become a "wounded healer" (the title of his first popular publication). We need to see each other as vulnerable, as open, as available, or else we cannot and will not confide in each other. We have to be willing to let our own faults and incapacities shine through because only then do others see us as fully and completely human. Henri was always willing to allow his own life to be such a vulnerable tool; he was beset by bouts of depression most of his life, and he chronicled his trials in his book, *The Inner Voice of Love.*

Third, everyone is a beloved child of God, even if they do not know it, and even if they refuse the honor. Hence, to really minister to one another, we have to learn how to elicit that beloved nature from one another. We have to learn what it means to be the beloved daughters and sons of God.

The model for this lavish love is the parable of the prodigal son in scripture (Luke 16) that has been written about by many commentators. Henri added his own twist to the commentary; he believed in the power of human touch to communicate the love of God. He wanted to embrace and be embraced by his friends and often declared his need to be bolstered up by an embrace.

Those who saw Henri as super-human found it hard to reconcile his vulnerability with their mistaken vision of him, but the point is clear: for Henri, the personal is the universal and the material bears the spiritual. As he wrote, "My hope is that the description of God's love in my life will give you the freedom and the courage to discover . . . God's love in yours." Thank you, Henri, for your example.

The Road to Love Goes Through Repentance

Christianity is the religion of love. That is what we say, and that is what many of us hold to as our reason for existence. We quote the passage in the Book of Acts: "see how these Christians love one another," which was unusual enough to be exemplary in an age of hostility and mistrust.

Christianity, this religion of loving our neighbor, proved hard to enact. Our history is besmirched by the demonization of others whom we were supposed to love. So it became easier over the centuries to kick the whole enterprise into heaven, so to speak, to spiritualize it and make our faith a highway to heaven rather than a roadmap for earth. We all know the caricature, that we Christians are more interested in the next life than in this one.

Contemplating love for our neighbor brings to mind the ancient church season of Lent, in which we anticipate the great festival of Easter. The full development of Lent was not complete until the fifth century, but the main components of the season were in place several centuries earlier. Some aspects of it came from the Gallican Church, some from the Roman, some from the East, but over time it was compiled as we know it today.

Two themes characterize Lent: learning and repentance. We call the learning "catechesis;" historically it is the way people enter the church at Easter time. You study aspects of the faith, sometimes in a formal setting, sometimes in conversation with your pastor. The point is to deepen your understanding, but for a purpose, not simply to learn "stuff." At its heart this learning aids you in knowing why you constantly shoot yourself in the foot morally and ethically, and offers you some tools to move past that experience.

The second theme of Lent, repentance, means to change our mind. It means to be sorry for our transgressions, of course, but at its core it means a change of mind. Learning and repentance go together; one leads to the other – and the point of both is to lead us deeper into love for God and into loving compassion toward others. This is consistent with Jesus' recitation of the two commandments of Judaism: to love God with all your heart, soul, and mind (the learning), and to love your neighbor as yourself (which is connected to repentance).

The more I learn about living the faith the more I know that I have to change my mind, turn around, and walk a different, renewed direction. We are all so full of pride, envy, greed, and the rest of the seven deadly sins that we have a consistent, virtually permanent, need for repentance. In one of our most-loved Orthodox prayers, we ask God to grant, "that we may spend our time in peace and repentance" – each condition being necessary for the other to thrive.

Of course, the signs of our need for repentance are carefully concealed when greed becomes a standard of living and pride is the fuel that powers much of our activity as people and as a nation.

The theory is that the more we undergo this turnaround involved in repentance, the more we will act out what we learn in our daily life. However, it is not just a theory. What actually happens when we seek someone's forgiveness for hurts we have inflicted? We open ourselves beyond pride, and we open a path to love again. In the Orthodox Christian tradition, Forgiveness Sunday marks the beginning of the Lenten season. Standing before each member of the congregation, we ask forgiveness for wrongs we have committed in the past year. This is not a perfunctory ritual; it continues to be among the deepest experiences people have in our church.

Not just during Lent, but at all times we can seek forgiveness from those we have hurt and repair our world (see page 19) through repentance.

SAINT BRENDAN

MAY 16

CHAPTER 8

Sent

ST BRENDAN

The Celtic Church distinguished three types of martyrdom. Red martyrs died for the faith, green (or blue) martyrs left the comforts of home to live as hermits or in community, and white martyrs were missionaries.

St Brendan, a shining example of white martyrdom, was born about 486 near Tralee, Ireland. He was raised by St Ita (see chapter one, in which she is given as an example of simplicity), and educated by her and the monks at her school in Killeedy. Brendan was ordained a monk by St Erc in 512 and would go on to become a founder of monasteries, mostly along the Shannon River, and most notably Clonfert, a major mission center.

St Brendan was a sailor. He embarked in 530 with a ship-load of monks in search of the so-called Blessed Isles, a mythic land of beauty lying "to the West" that was mentioned by Plato. "The Voyage of Brendan the Abbot," a ninth century document, tells us that in this seven-year journey, he made it as far as America. Who knows? It is widely accepted that Columbus read it before he set sail; the book was fairly well-known throughout late medieval Europe, especially through a 12th century Dutch translation.

Although it has some amazing speculations attached to it, Brendan's missionary zeal exceeds the fanciful legend of his sea voyage. Long thought to be essentially a monastic tale, in recent decades there have been discoveries in Newfoundland and the Northeast of the U.S. that suggest Brendan might indeed have made it that far. Navigators who have followed the seaways recorded in the *Navigatio* have found them to be accurate descriptions of the trip.

Brendan's mission work is legendary. He established the See of Ardfert, a monastery in County Clare. Scholars believe he then visited Wales and Scotland, particularly the monastery at Iona, before returning home around 557 to found his most famous settlement, Clonfert Monastery.

From his base at Clonfert, St Brendan became a sort of pied piper for people interested in mission work who were attracted by his expansive spirit. It is said that thousands of monks went forth from Clonfert to carry the message of the cross and resurrection to people all over the known world, inspired by his spirit of mission and adventure. He died at his sister Briga's monastery at Annaghdown in 577.

St Brendan has rightfully been called "a wanderer for Christ." Endowed with a missionary's heart, he was willing to search for others with whom to share the Christian faith. He did not seek captive audiences, nor did he force his faith on others. We can safely assume that he learned much about the people whom he visited, using that knowledge as a means to speak to them of Christ and his work.

It is important to those of us who have more regulated and time-bound lives to realize that Brendan was essentially carefree in his wanderings, guided only by the love of Christ, a curiosity about the world and its people, and a spirit of adventure. In a sense, the mission came to him rather than via him following an agenda governed by maps or commissions.

The monastery at Clonfert did not survive a final attack in 1541, during the period known as the Dissolution under King Henry VIII. Nevertheless, the Cathedral of St Brendan, Ireland's oldest living church, remains active at Clonfert. Surely Brendan is a navigator for our times as well as his own: an adventurer willing to risk new voyages for his faith. We commemorate him on May 16.

TROPAR

Thine angelic life of fasting hath spread thy glory
throughout the Church of Christ,
O venerable Father Brendan.
For thou didst sail the waters of the
thundering sea,
Like a merchant seeking a pearl of great price,
But didst obtain it in the heavens from the hand
of thy Lord.
Wherefore, O God-bearing father,
Bestow this treasure upon those who now call
upon thee with faith,
And who cherish thine honored memory.

What the Celts Contributed to Mission

One of the Celtic secrets was, and should still be, an emphasis on community in the midst of evangelism, and the evangelistic outreach of the community. Just as we are not Christian alone, so we are called to common witness.

The rudimentary organization of early Celtic communities was the basis for the infectious spread of Christian faith, especially in Wales and Ireland. Small communities of people living together and sharing the tasks of life were the model for the Christian community as well. The monastery was the village, so to speak, even as today the local church is the village that raises its children in the faith. Drop out of the village and you are unlikely to continue to grow in its values. It's as simple – and as profound – as that.

In his book *The Celtic Way of Evangelism*, teacher George G. Hunter III underlines the great difference between the institutional and the communal approaches to the faith. The community was, in his words, "more imaginative and less cerebral, closer to nature and its creatures, and emphasized the 'immanence' and 'providence' of the Triune God more than his 'transcendence.'"

There is a line in the Psalms – perhaps more than one – that talks about "setting the solitary in families." God's desire and intent for humanity is community, not isolation. We learn solitude not necessarily by being solitary. The function of a monastery is to teach the brothers or sisters (or both) over time how to be alone in community. Conversely, we learn how to be in community while we are alone. This mystery, though inexplicable, remains true.

So we discover God not only inwardly in the midst of our solitude, but also outwardly in the midst of a community. But that community must be focused on God. Scripture makes a nice distinction between the laity and the crowd. The crowd may function as a mob. There has always been mob hysteria, to use the old term. But that mob is unfocused, unwashed, and unforgiven. In the *laos*, to use the Greek term from which we get the word laity, there is cohesion, bonding, and focus.

The difference between crowd and laity is outward, rather than inward focus. A crowd may be whipped up about its agenda, but the agenda remains outside itself. In the laity of the Christian community, there is unity of purpose and common direction. (Read the Epistle to the Ephesians, especially the fourth chapter, for further indications of how this works.)

I am always thrilled when I can lead classes for people contemplating entry into Orthodox Christianity. A bond forms among those gathered, and the commonality of movement toward a goal makes for a sense of united pilgrimage, a sense one hopes remains after people actually enter into the faith through the "awe-inspiring rites of initiation." Even in long-distance classes, I invite people to share their inquiries with one another because knowledge is gained through the conversations that take place in camaraderie.

Conversely, some of the people I have seen come and go in the church are those for whom the common bonds never really came to fruition, and in whom generosity toward others was not inspired. The engine of social consciousness was not assembled as they became Orthodox. They drifted off without a deep sense of commitment within community.

Following the Celts' communal approach to the faith, we have it in a nutshell: all outreach flows from the initial emphasis. If we emphasize our nearness to God in words and actions, it is infectious, like the love people have for the down-to-earth prayers of the peasants that Alexander Carmichael recorded in the *Carmina Gadelica*. We hear a song of faith rather than a set of dogmas. We see love of others in action. We learn the faith by osmosis, not by drill. It is a gift of the Celtic church.

Going Forth in Peace: A Christmas Meditation for the Entire Year

Some years it is tough to talk about Christmas as the festival of peace, and Christ as the Prince of Peace. We look around us and what do we see but wars, rumors of war, strife, hideous torment, and horrific slaughter, as if human life has no meaning, purpose, or dignity. The cheapening of human and animal life goes against every fiber of our being and consciousness.

We seem to be drifting farther away rather than nearer to the ideal of Peace that Christmas offers. We sense that we are immersed in a universe that is indifferent to our existence – maybe not hostile, but in any evident sense impersonal, uncaring, not even noticing that we exist. It is enough to make us callous and cynical.

So . . . let us start at the beginning once again. Let us realize that Christmas is not automatically a celebration of peace. Even in our homes, the demonic urges that infest our world lead to an increase in domestic violence at this time of year. If we want the season to be a celebration of peace, then we have to make it so.

We must be "sober and vigilant" for, indeed, the enemy is "walking about like a roaring lion seeking to devour someone" (I Peter 5:8). The Apostle Paul says that we fight "not against flesh and blood but against powers and principalities." That is the ancient way to talk about forces that appear to be beyond our control. Paul teaches that Christ overcame these powers and principalities; because of his victory we are no longer at the mercy of forces beyond our control. This applies to the simplest forces, like being governed by stars, to the most complex, that the politics and ravages of war will overcome us.

St Seraphim of Sarov (1754-1833), one of my heroes of the faith, lived the truth that the powers and principalities have already been overcome. He did not do great and mighty things, what he did was live a faithful life in the midst of trials. He counseled many people, and he himself became a destination for pilgrims. His most famous saying, which we display on a mural in our home, is "Acquire the spirit of peace and thousands around you will be saved."

We can interpret St Seraphim's saying a number of ways. First, if we acquire the spirit of peace we will be so peaceful that others will find their peace in us. Second, there exists a spirit of peace; if we tap into it, we will find that spirit. Third, the spirit of peace is available to thousands if they find its source. It is not in me, personally, but I may exhibit it in some small way.

I don't think it matters much which interpretation we take, including coming up with our own. The main point is that peace is a *creation*. Peace is not a state we enter, but rather a pathway we have to clear through the minefields of stress, hostility, and hatred.

Jesus Christ brought peace on the cross and at the resurrection. As a believer, the spirit of peace is a reality I have to create ... one step at a time.

But the Greatest of these is Charity

Every Wednesday, Dr. Hittner, our high school principal, would begin the all-school assembly program with a selected reading from the Bible. This was the Fifties, in one of the largest high schools in Pennsylvania. Nobody was excused. Boys came in trousers, wearing dress shirts and ties, no t-shirts allowed. Girls wore skirts and blouses. Each assembly was opened with the Pledge of Allegiance, the Bible passages were read without comment, and then the program began.

Dr. Hittner avoided Bible passages considered doctrinaire or sectarian, so we heard many Psalms and, occasionally, readings from the Books of Isaiah or Micah. From the New Testament, he read I Corinthians 13, Paul's magnificent hymn to "faith, hope, and charity." We heard it somewhat regularly, maybe three or four times a year, since it was one of only a few New Testament chapters he favored.

The passage from I Corinthians has stuck in my mind ever since as a sort of religion-neutral encouragement to be compassionate. Because of that high school experience, I always link it with Micah, chapter 6, with its passionate injunction, "What does the Lord require of you but to do justice, love kindness, and walk humbly with your God?" Justice and compassion. They belong together in everyone's walk through this world – no matter what our "race, color, or creed."

In contemplating I Corinthians 13 recently – "for the greatest of these is charity" – I was struck by something that has lain hidden in my consciousness all these years. It was sparked by comments of St Augustine, the great bishop and theologian in the fourth and fifth centuries. Referring to this passage, Augustine says that faith and hope will disappear beyond this life, but charity will remain. His reasons are twofold: we will not need faith, because our faith will either be confirmed or not, and thus will pass away. We will not need hope because the object of our hope will have been achieved, that being the vision of God granted to the blessed.

So hope will pass away, and knowledge, too, for "it will cease." But charity, or love – ah, that is different – for it will remain. Augustine's conclusion is simple: "The three virtues of faith, hope, and charity are necessary for this life; but after this life, charity alone will suffice." As Paul says, imperfect things pass away, but love? That never passes away.

This is a sobering thought. It means that the arguments people spend so much time on, the arguments that can proceed even to the level of violence by one believer against another, will not be worth a hill of beans once we are gone. Returning to the words of the Prophet Micah, we learn that what counts is to "do justice, love kindness, and walk humbly with your God." After this life is over, and no matter what may lie beyond it, the main event will have been the justice we pursued and the love we poured out toward others.

When we die we will probably *not* say, "Gee if only I had gone to one more meeting or scored one more business deal." What will count will be the selfless love we showed to others. The medieval classic *The Imitation of Christ* rests on this thought. We are not called to imitate the faith or the hope of Christ, if we are Christians, but his love and compassion. That is where the path leads. To express love and compassion is at once more human and more divine than all of our knowledge and faith and hope.

Keeping the Door Open

The beginning of the year is always a time of assessment. Along with many others, I feel compelled to ask myself if my pathway continues to make sense, or if I need to shift course. It is the same with my approach to faith. I am unable to simply put the facts in my back pocket and walk on from there as if there was nothing new to be learned, no new experiences that will challenge and perhaps even alter my faith. I want to make sure that there is an opening for this aspect of my life.

One of my favorite poets is Czeslaw Milosz, who said in his 1980 Nobel Lecture, "The exile of a poet is today a simple function of a relatively recent discovery; that whoever wields power is also able to control language, and not only with the prohibition of censorship, but also by changing the meaning of words." Milosz says that the task of the poet is to keep open "whole zones of reality" that are in danger of being closed. And not only poets, but this can also refer to those who speak clearly of God through the Tradition we have embraced.

In the West, the forces of godlessness have been unleashed, not yet with fury, but surely with firmness. Religion fades not yet through oppression, but already through trivialization. The great difficulty is that few people know the Tradition which gave birth to centuries of philosophy, art, and culture. Thus they are vulnerable to winds of teaching that have no grounding. Fifty years ago Martin Luther King could assume that people knew the voice of the Prophets when he used their words to underline his position and movement. Today this knowledge has dwindled to the point that, as mission thinker George W. Hunter III has put it, we are in the age of the new barbarians.

Toward the end of Milosz's life (he died in 2004), he said that we had entered the new age of homelessness. He did not use the word in the usual way; he meant that because of shifts in our self-understanding, we all find ourselves without a home. We do not fit in the universe any more. There is no friendliness, no embrace, no sense of belonging. We have become drifters on a cosmic plane, too small and insignificant to make any difference.

This homelessness is what the forces of faith oppose.

As the tides of atheism rise, we should not run away. Instead, we should welcome opportunities for dialogue. The tradition of the our faith is deep and broad, essentially inexhaustible, and definitely capable of wrestling with angels and demons alike. We have a long history of reasoned faith to ingest and fall back on. Let us not lose hope, but rather make sure that we are each doing our part to keep open that zone of reality which is in danger of eclipse.

Creative Imagining, Interpretation, and God

I have always been fascinated by the way the Old Testament demolished the mythology upon which some of its stories was based. The creation is a prime example. The two creation stories in the Genesis account have been fused together by a creative editor. In neither one does the mythic basis get more than a passing reference. All the gods were reduced to natural forces and only one Creator of everything remains.

In mythologies current in the second millennium BCE, at least in the myths roundabout Israel, the gods are themselves at the service of external forces. They are not in charge of the creation and chaos reigns supreme. The gods are not totally powerful, nor are they singular. There is no monotheism. The stories are full of magic and divination, with multiple deities roaming the mythic landscape like Tolkien creatures. The writers of the Old Testament stories ransacked contemporary mythology and dragooned it into the service of the imagination.

Even for non-believers there could be some appeal in the Old Testament's depiction of one Creator God, when we consider the background against which the narrative was created or compiled, and how the editors have altered it.

There are other places in the Jewish and Christian scriptures that explore this imaginative interpretation. Two examples are the infancy narratives in the Gospels of Matthew and Luke, and the wonderfully imaginative first chapter of the Gospel of John.

It is especially the potential appeal to others that makes me raise the issue of myth and the uses of the imagination in interpretation. When it comes to understanding the three-letter word GOD and whatever meaning that three-letter word might hold, we need the imagination.

The German philosopher Immanuel Kant called imagination the power to recall and reconstruct absent events.

Memory is the repository, but imagination is the creative act of the mind. Students of English literature usually learn Samuel Taylor Coleridge's distinction between fancy and imagination from his *Biographia Literaria*. Primary imagination is a "repetition in the finite mind of the eternal act of creation in the infinite I AM." Secondary imagination recreates what primary imagination gives us. Fancy is essentially passive, repetitive, and mechanical.

The imagination, both primary and secondary, offers us meanings that we cannot communicate through proposition or logic. It is active and creative, and expresses our human potential. In other words, some meanings *only* emerge through story or poetry; we only get them through those forms.

So then, we can only communicate the content of the three-letter word GOD *via* our imaginative interpretation of the data of our lives. And that is what the interpreters *within* scripture are doing, with regard to the Creation or the person known as Jesus. They are using the imagination to convey to others the meaning of God or, perhaps better, to create a meaning for the word that will convey something of its reality without defining it, since every act of definition is a limitation. They know that to define it is to lose it, because if the word God means anything at all, it refers to a personal power that cannot be grasped, only held in awesome reverence. This truth is exceedingly tough to take for people who want everything nailed down, but it remains true.

Just as each of us needs to be able to exceed the limits of the definitions others put upon us, so also does God. And just as we use imagination to get out of the boxes that trap us, so imagination is the tool to free God from being our hostage, to explore God with new eyes.

Starting Once Again from the Beginning

If you search the New Testament you will find the church there from the beginning, even before the New Testament was written. Most people are aware that Paul wrote his letters before any Gospel was written; so, for that matter, did Peter. The Gospels came at least a generation, maybe more, after the church began as a movement with leaders known as priests (or "elders"), deacons, and overseers (bishops). These roles were not late additions, but part of the original movement, as one can see from a quick glance at Acts chapter 6.

The question might now occur, what is the church for? Again, search the New Testament and you find a number of roles the church plays as part of its warrant. Chief among these is worship, followed closely by witness, teaching, service, and fellowship. Teaching and fellowship strengthen the church inwardly so that we might engage in witness and service.

That word witness in Greek is *martyria*, and from it comes the name for those who gave their lives in times of persecution. There are martyrs today in many countries around the world. We must remember them and continue to remind our government that they exist, for they are often forgotten.

The heart of the church, however, remains worship. The Greek word for this is *leitourgia*, "liturgy," which remains the name of the chief Sunday service in Orthodox Christianity today. Other churches also use it. A composite word, it means "the work of the people." Note that: the work of the people. It is not the work of one person who stands up front and speaks. It is not the work of a small choir which sings special music. It is the work of the *people*, all of us together. For instance, in the Orthodox Church, we cannot hold a Divine Liturgy with just a priest. We need a community of about ten at a minimum to fulfill all the roles in worship, and we can expand the number beyond that with ease. Worshiping together is participatory and not a show. We are not here to sink into ourselves, but to be drawn outside ourselves into the larger realm signified by God.

The heart of liturgy, then, is a conversation between God and humanity. Our part of the conversation involves prayer and praise and thanksgiving. God's part of the conversation involves the *Word* both read from scripture and then proclaimed, and the *Mysteries* we call by various names: baptism, Holy Communion, forgiveness, and so forth. These are the ways God comes to us.

Note that this is a bodily experience, not merely one of hearing. Without both halves of the conversation we are diminished. And both halves have been there since the beginning, as we see in the books of Acts, I Corinthians, and Ephesians.

Why bother to rehearse this?

First, because of the tragedies of religious history, many churches lost part of the conversation. The Reformation in the Western church cut off so much of the complete ancient liturgy that it was in danger of losing the heart of worship. Thankfully many Reformation churches have re-created the liturgy in these latter days.

Secondly, I am concerned to find the proper setting between a view that the church has no reason for being and that it is the be-all and end-all of our existence. The church is a vehicle, not a destination; it is an organism, not an institution. It has a specific purpose, to worship, and worship has the specific purpose of enlarging us as people by locating us in the heart of God. In that mode we live our daily lives of service and compassion.

That the body of Christ is the church and that the body of Christ is the Eucharist: these are not two truths, but only one. This one truth is at the heart of Celtic spirituality. This one truth needs to be recognized and revived for us to see and feel and touch the deep meaning of church. This is church beyond the walls of a building, liturgy as the genuine work of the people, and assembly as that which constitutes our very existence as people. We are not in this alone. This is the heart of the Celtic understanding – the experience – of the Christian community.

9

SAINT DAVID

MARCH 1

CHAPTER 9

Sanctity

ST DAVID

St David, or Dewi Sant, as he is known in Wales, reposed in the year 589. Tradition holds that he was born in Henvynyw in Cardiganshire, Wales. His mother was the holy woman Non, who was sainted and famous in her own right in both Wales and Brittany. His father was the king Sanctus, whose name befits that man's faithfulness as well. Rhygyfarch, author and compiler of the *Life of St David*, says that his birth was surrounded by natural wonders, in particular a thunderstorm of great intensity. This is, of course, a way of saying that David was in some sense a "second Christ", at least to the Welsh people.

David began his life in the church as a monk at the monastery called Yr Henllwyn ("the old grove"). He showed a deep love for Christ and the church which manifested itself in a life of holiness, characterized by simplicity and charity toward others.

David spent a decade in training at Yr Henllwyn, learning the psalms, the hymnody of the church, worship life, and leadership. His developing passion for the faith led him into mission work. In this, he joined many other Celtic saints who followed the threefold path of martyrdom which included wandering for the sake of planting the faith, known as the "white martyrdom."

According to Rhygyfarch, St David founded no less than a dozen monasteries as far afield as Glastonbury and Bath. He founded his first monastery near his birthplace. In time, it became the site for the 12th century Cathedral of St David. The town now bears his name and the cathedral is the site of a pilgrimage on March 1st each year.

David's sanctity is demonstrated by his asceticism. He taught the monks of his monasteries to live an austere life, spending most of the day in silence. They drank no wine, eating primarily vegetables and precious little meat – and that was mostly in the form of fish. Because leeks were a plentiful and regular part of their diet, they eventually became a symbol for Wales itself and remain the national plant to this day.

No written rule survives from St David's monasteries, but we can infer that it was similar to the austere rules that governed other monasteries of the Celtic leaders like Columba or Gildas, which in turn were grounded in the approach of St Anthony of the Desert and St John Cassian, whose rule brought Anthony's influence to the west.

St David's approach to sanctity, however austere, freed him and his monks for charitable works. Rhygyfarch is lavish in his praise for the work of David in "caring for the brethren" and "feeding a multitude of orphans, wards, widows, needy, sick, feeble and pilgrims. So he started, so he continued, and so he ended." According to tradition, he lived for over 100 years, and reposed on Tuesday, March 1st in 589. It is said that his monastery was "filled with angels as Christ received his soul."

David's reputation is based on his kindness, compassion, and understanding of the needs of others. There is no record of violence or even harshness on his part. Indeed, he cared for "the little things" of life, by which he seems to have meant those attitudes and actions that bind society together in unity under God. This is holiness or sanctity at a very primary and basic level, a level from which we can all learn.

Interestingly, St David has not always been the patron saint of Wales. That honor was originally bestowed on St Gwenfrewi (see chapter four). When her relics were translated from Holywell to Shrewsbury and, thus, outside the borders of Wales, the honor was transferred to St David, on whom it rests to this day. St David's day is March 1.

TROPAR

> *Having worked miracles in thy youth,*
> *Founded monasteries and converted the pagans*
>   *who had sought to destroy thee,*
> *O Father David,*
> *Christ our God blessed thee to receive the episco-*
>   *pate at the place of His Resurrection.*
> *Intercede for us,*
> *That our lives may be blessed and our souls may*
>   *be saved.*

Being Good or Being Holy: Living the Difference

For years I have heard people say that being Christian is about being good or ethical. Simply put, that is not, and has never been true. In fact, I have no beef with people who say that atheists make better ethical decisions than do some Christians. My objection is that being Christian is not the same thing as being good.

Everyone can find ways to be good, although in our fallen world it is nearly miraculous that we coexist with as little friction and violence as we do. As much mayhem as there is, I marvel daily that there is not more. However, the "goodness" argument is a diversion.

If Christianity is not about goodness, then what is it about? It is a spiritual path to holiness.

I can hear you thinking, "Holiness? What an outdated or misused word!" But consider this. Holiness has several meanings, none of which is "goodie two-shoes" or "holier-than-thou." Those slurs are also a diversion, deliberately meant to throw us off the path.

Holiness can be defined in two ways. First, *separateness* – the idea of separating from what is unholy or, in other words, profane or obscene. Profanity originally meant naughty acts outside the *fanum* (the temple where the holy action is) rather than inside. It meant to defile or disrespect religious acts. To be holy is to be consecrated, set apart from that which is obscene or profane.

Holiness also means to be involved in the sacred rituals – which may include what we think of as "religious services," but need not. Sacredness is primarily in the act, not in the locale, which is secondary and a reminder that all of life is to be lived as if you were in the temple. That is why obscenity occurs "offstage," *outside* the temple, and was unspoken onstage in ancient times.

A second stream of meaning is visible in Anglo-Saxon words; health, healing, holiness, and wholeness all connect both linguistically and in reality. Holiness means to be healthy and whole, which in past ages always meant that one related healthfully to God, to creation, to others, and ultimately to oneself. It concerns physical and spiritual health and achieving balance.

With that foundation, we can now see why the search for holiness is life-long. Holiness is not a matter of believing a handful of things we hold intellectually; it requires commitment for the long haul, rather like marriage. It is a way and not a belief system, a walk and not a station. It is not mental so much as it is physical. As Chaucer (following Hippocrates) said of love, (for Hippocrates, medicine) so we can say of holiness: "the life so short, the craft so long to learn."

If we define holiness as the search for wholeness through consecration and commitment to a respectful, spiritual way of being in the world, we see the two meanings converge.

Christians speak of developing the "mind of Christ" (Colossians 3). This is not a form of intelligence so much as it is a way to see the world. "All religion is but a looking," said the French seeker Simone Weil. She was a deeply holy person who saw that the faith she pursued leads to wholeness because it enables us to see the world from the perspective of eternity.

When we take the long view, so to speak, many of the concerns that plague us and throw us off balance recede to the background of our lives. Paradoxically, we are then enabled to concentrate on that which is in front of us, to pay attention and enter into the moment in a whole and holy way.

Learning Spiritual Virtues on the Road

Spiritual virtues are best learned on the ground. The Christian approach locates spirituality in ordinary existence. God entered the human mainstream, so we learn about and experience divine matters through material pathways. Since there is no distant religious universe separated from our normal life, we need not escape this world to experience holiness. If God became human, it stands to reason that we can know God's presence and meaning, and experience spiritual virtues, in everyday life.

To illustrate this, here is my tale.

We are driving home from California after vacation with family, when the car suddenly overheats. We pull off at Eloy, Arizona, a town trying to come back after Interstate 10 bypassed it. The local motel has a business card for "Mike's Automotive." It is 5:30, but he is open until 6:30. So we limp the car over to Mike's.

We enter a corrugated metal building with car parts covering the walls. It looks like the junk bin in the Death Star from Star Wars. Hispanic pop music is the soundtrack for the five guys working on cars. In all, a visually perfect setting: exactly the kind of castle in which you would expect your local expert mechanic to reign. Mike (or Miguel, his given name) looks at our car immediately.

The spiritual virtue in view here is patience. Mike has it. He orders the fan clutch, we stay overnight. It arrives by noon, he quickly installs it, and we are on our way.

Twenty miles east of Eloy, the car overheats again. We call Mike. He says, "Bring it back immediately." The options for the problem expand, but this is a man who knows his craft. We watch him try every penultimate solution. He again exhibits patience as he runs through various possibilities, testing them, moving on to each new proposal.

It is a joy to watch Mike work. We take the car out for test runs, and each time it fails the test and overheats. We are disappointed and so is Mike, but he is undaunted. He must find the problem. He ultimately discerns that we need a new radiator. The suspense builds as Mike drives 45 miles to pick up the last available one for our make and year, only to have to drive another 18 miles when it is not there as promised. He arrives at the second store four minutes before closing, then returns to us. By 11:00 PM we are on the road, the car purring through the night to the Mesilla Valley. Sunrise over the Organs never looked so good.

While he was testing different options under the hood, I said, "Mike you're an artist." "No," he said, "I'm more like a surgeon." I suggested that his virtue was patience. He agreed. "You have to be patient or else you might overlook the one thing that will solve the problem," he said. "You can't give up."

Using this experience to think about patience, we see that it has different components: *curiosity* about the source of the problem, *willingness* to test different options, *risking* failure without giving up, and, above all, *tenacity*. Mike was determined to find that problem, even if it consumed all his time, because he wanted to get us back on the road.

We may be tempted to say that this is simply an example of someone trying to help. But I see it as the demonstration of a spiritual virtue. I spoke with Mike about his patience as a spiritual virtue, and he agreed, though he was humble about acknowledging it. After all, he was "just doing his job." But this lesson will long stick with me. I am grateful for the virtue of patience he demonstrated on our behalf. And I still think he was an artist.

Humor and the Spiritual Life

Years ago I put a series of "hooks" on my office door. They were poignant notes, intended to make passersby do a double take. The most popular posting read, "Some people say it's sacrilegious to make fun of your religion. Personally, I think it's the only way to be religious." I hoped my visitors caught the irony in my humorous comment.

In the 1960s, the Quaker philosopher Elton Trueblood wrote a book called *The Humor of Christ*. One of the first people to explore the territory, he drew attention to many places in the gospel that could be understood more readily if seen as humorous, or at least ironic. For instance, consider the exchange between Jesus and a woman he refuses to cure. He seems to insult her by saying, "It isn't right to give the children's food to the dogs." This seems like a shocking comment, doesn't it, coming from Jesus? But Trueblood argues that Jesus was teasing her. And the woman seems to understand, because she makes a great comeback: "Yes, but even the dogs eat the scraps that fall from the table." We can imagine Jesus smiling or even laughing at her retort, as if to say, "If you can make a comeback like that, of course I will heal you."

There is a certain irony, in fact, that in the late Sixties and early Seventies – a gentler time when a lot of social commentary and action was playful – there was a spate of books that explored the gospel as comedy. Some of these books pointed out that in earlier centuries the church celebrated days like the "Feast of Fools," when bishops became choirboys and choirboys became bishops for a day. This humorous irony showed that perhaps the arrangement of power relations on earth does not reflect what is true or makes good sense "in heaven," so to speak. Here we see the church acting as court jester, commissioned to stick needles in the balloons that mark our pretensions and arrogance of power.

We often use humor to deflate the pompous and uplift the lowly. This use of humor has a great history in social, political, and religious circles. Yet so many Christians look sad, depressed, and downright miserable. Could it be that we take ourselves too seriously?

It is possible to take the world seriously, on one hand, and yet underline its foibles through humor, on the other hand. Jesus seems to have done both. As the writer of Ecclesiastes might have said, there is a time for seriousness and there is a time for humor. Both have their place in spiritual life.

We need comic relief from time to time. A hearty laugh at the foibles of humanity is good for the soul. Jesus saw this in his humorous saying about pompous religionists, *"You are blind guides, who strain out a gnat and swallow a camel whole!"* (Matthew 23:24). Who could not guffaw at such a comparison?

Is it going too far to say that the gospel can be comedy? Doesn't it end with the crucifixion of Christ, one of the tragic moments in history? Well, yes, there is death, and we do well not to overlook it. But for Christians, the tragic note is not the end. The resurrection of Christ is God's great comic surprise that breaks history and offers new life and purpose. This may not be ordinary humor, but it's the sort of humor the prophets and Jesus might have enjoyed. It is the humor of the gospel over the long range; namely, that God trumps all.

A Holy Face is a Beautiful Face

The beauty of holiness is in the face of a nun. Beauty untouched by any artificial, chemical, or cosmetic means can stun us, especially if costuming prevents us from viewing the rest of the body. When we are limited to the face, we see with an intensity that eludes us if there is more to observe. It is like being deprived of one of our senses; our remaining faculties are heightened. Seeing this figure robed in black except for the oval of her face, we see more than if she were clothed in what we call normal attire.

The beauty of holiness in the face of a nun is ageless. Age has not only its privilege, but also its unique beauty, and the beauty of holiness is evident in people of all ages.

When we spend time with nuns (and monks, too, for they also have a particular appeal when they are robed in black), an open intimacy draws us into their world and allows us to speak freely and confidentially, making us feel as if we are the only two who exist in this moment. That must be the reason why it feels natural and right and easy to engage in spiritual conversation with monastics. The accoutrements of ordinary life are swept away; that is the gentle power of the habit.

What purpose do these monastics serve? Many see them as useless and outmoded in this digital age. Not so. Bishop Alexander Golitzin, a contemporary Orthodox leader, reminds us that monks and nuns are scandalous, charismatic, and prophetic.

The nun is *scandalous* because she points toward a future not yet unfolded into the present; namely, the future of God. With no morbid touch, this unfolding future is what death holds: the promise of release from the cares of life, the promise of eternal rest – but in this life. The nun anticipates that end by shunning the material trappings and possessions that bog most of us down.

The nun is *charismatic* because she lives in the light of those gifts the Spirit promises to the faithful: love, joy, peace, patience, and wisdom. Beholden to none, she can be present and free for all. Her spirit is captive to no agenda, time, place, or conflicting commitments.

The nun is *prophetic* because she speaks for God in her attitude, her demeanor, her thoughts, and her activities. The prophet is not an oracle or a fortuneteller. The prophet proposes by his or her speech, thought, and deeds that alternative spiritual path that leads to and proceeds from God.

These days, most of us Westerners do not apprehend the point of monastics. They pass us by unnoticed, or possibly as an irritant or challenge. In the old world, however, they are still sought out for counsel and companionship because people know the secret characteristics they show forth. People know that the beauty of holiness resides in their faces even as the holiness of beauty resides in their person.

Monasteries, and the monastics within them, continue to be a magnet for many who seek honesty of spirit, natural humanity, and the beauty of holiness. Even after the monasteries have ceased to be vital, the holiness remains, and people continue to visit places like Holy Island and Shrewsbury, in Celtic lands.

Blessing All Things Bright and Beautiful

If you were to look at their prayer books, it might appear as if Jews bless God for things and events, whereas Christians bless things and events for God.

That approach is, indeed, too simplistic, so I would go on from there to explain. The truth is that we Christians, also, bless God for stuff. Many of our Christian prayers begin, *Baruch atah Adonai*, Blessed is our God.

Blessing is a major duty for Orthodox parish priests, because blessings are a vehicle to the spiritual interconnection of all things. This is encouraged by The Ecumenical Patriarch of Orthodox Christianity, in his concern for the environment and campaign for a return to a more earthy spirituality.

A significant example of this is the season of house blessings, which we begin at Theophany (Epiphany in the West), early in each new year. Theophany is when Orthodox Christians commemorate the baptism of Jesus at the hands of John the Baptizer. House blessings extend over the weeks from

Theophany through Candlemas, when we commemorate Mary's rite of purification after childbirth.

In our house blessings, we constantly refer to the concept that Christ, by entering the water of the Jordan at baptism, blessed all waters. This extends to the water we use to bless the rooms of the houses of our people. It is also the reason we bless the waters where we live. And when one lives in the desert as we do, this becomes an especially meaningful gesture.

Besides house blessings, many parishes also sponsor a yearly blessing of the animals. At our parish, we get a lot of dogs. Few cats are interested, but one year a miniature horse and some goats appeared. The prayers for this blessing are ancient, and we locate the festival on the church calendar around the days of St Seraphim of Sarov, St Anthony of the Desert our patron, both of whom are noted in Orthodox tradition for their closeness to animals. St Seraphim is often depicted with Misa, his friend among the bears, and on one icon of St Anthony, heaven is depicted with deer, rabbits, cranes, and other animals among the trees and shrubbery. We have since added St Melangell (whom see at the beginning of chapter three). In a switch from the usual pattern, we ask the animals to bless God for their being, in accordance with the *Canticle of the Three Youths in the Fiery Furnace* (from the Septuagint).

Another blessing at the beginning of the year is *Tu Bishvat*, a Jewish holiday that commemorates the return of fertility to the land of Israel. It is also known as the "New Year of the Trees." There is no theological connection to *Theophany*, but the spiritual connection joins us in concern for the earth and all that is therein.

Blessing is grounded in gratitude and topped with thanksgiving. It spreads our awareness onto a broad vista, and is more an attitude than an aspect of religion.

If we take it seriously, blessing has the potential to become a way of life. For a direct line connects blessing my dogs to my awareness of the greed that consumes the environment rapaciously. A direct line connects the blessing of the rooms in my house to concern for domestic life in general; a house in which rooms have been blessed must not become a scene of domestic violence. A direct line connects blessing local waters to my consciousness about water in general, and indeed the preciousness of all natural resources.

Blessing is *expansive*. Blessing is *inclusive*. Blessing relates to real life. May you be blessed.

The Virtue of Excellence has Many Shades

Among the ancient Greeks, excellence was considered the primary virtue. It was the grounding for all other qualities that we think of as virtues, like justice, courage, prudence, and temperance – or faith, hope, and love. Homer, author of the *Odyssey* and the *Iliad,* used the word to describe military valor or any social performance of a high level.

It is always difficult to translate Greek for which, as in all languages, words have many shades of meaning, and "excellence" is no exception. The list of possible translations includes righteousness, asceticism, wisdom, and faithfulness.

Let us begin with "righteousness." Leaving aside any negative connotations the word may have picked up like barnacles, righteousness may be defined as "doing the right thing," as in the Spike Lee movie of the same name. We want to do good because we are good, or at least seek to be good. As Einstein memorably said, "Try not to become a man of success. Try to become a man of value." He had the right idea, or the idea of rightness. Righteousness and excellence are joined at the hip, so to speak. The one involves the other. But let us explore other shades of meaning.

The virtue of excellence connects with another value in ancient Greek society, one that shows up in the New Testament (as does "excellence"). That value is represented by asceticism. This may surprise you, but if we delve into the word, you will understand my point.

The word asceticism did not originally call up visions of monks starving themselves half to death to fulfill a spiritual ideal, or performing odd feats like living on top of pillars as a witness against their society. Originally asceticism simply meant "training," physical and mental training for an athletic contest, like the Olympics. It is probably no accident that the ancient Greeks, for whom excellence was the primary virtue, invented games for which they would train hard, and at which they could test their mettle to demonstrate excellence.

St Paul speaks about training for Christian faith using words shaped for athletic training in I Corinthians 9:24-26. We train to win the prize, which in this context is the ability to hold to the gospel and communicate its meaning to other people (people like the Corinthians, who were a tough crowd to play to).

Another shade of meaning for excellence is wisdom, or good thinking. Frankly, there seems to be an anti-intellectual streak in American Christianity that flies in the face of the search for this kind of excellence. Instead, it is as if there were some cockamamie value in doing things ineptly, and without grace and style. Given that attitude, we can hardly blame people who pass Christianity by, when we do not seem to be striving for excellence.

Yet another facet of excellence is faithfulness in our way of living. During the 2012 Summer Olympics in London, a compelling photograph of three Russian woman gymnasts lighting prayer candles at the Orthodox Cathedral of the Dormition and All Saints, Ennismore Gardens, appeared. These young women trained intensely for years to become excellent gymnasts, but they also attended the Divine Liturgy in the midst of the Olympics. Their spiritual practice nurtured their physical excellence, and vice versa. They were still themselves, whether as excellent gymnasts or as Orthodox Christians. These young women exhibited faithfulness – not for the camera, but for themselves.

The pursuit of excellence is a spiritual quest. The pathways converge: athletics, intellectual endeavors, spiritual disciplines – they all lead to excellence. The ancient Greeks and early Christians understood this, and we, too, are invited to the quest. Let us not spurn the invitation.

Theosis: Growing in Faith and Life

Theosis means deification or divinization. The concept stems from II Peter 1:3, 4: "His divine power has given us every-thing we need for a godly life through our knowledge of him who called us by his own glory and goodness. Through these he has given us his very great and precious promises, so that through them you may participate in the divine nature, having escaped the corruption in the world caused by evil desires."

Theosis means, in the words of St Anastasios of Sinai: " . . . the elevation to what is better, but not the reduction of our nature to something less, nor is it a change in our human nature. . . . That which is of God is that which has been lifted up to a greater glory, without its own nature being changed."

Theosis is our restoration to the image of God (Genesis 1, 2), but many of the fathers insist that it is a restoration beyond the original image. This is because we now move into the image of Christ through the power of the Spirit, enacted in the Body of Christ, the church. Theosis brings us into the Uncreated Light of Mount Tabor that shone through Christ at the Transfiguration (Mark 9:2ff). Living in this Light transforms us into the image of Christ.

We can trace a line straight from Paul to St Irenaeus in the second century, who wrote of "the Word of God, our Lord Jesus Christ, who did, through his transcendent love, become what we are, that He might bring us to be even what He is Himself" (*Against Heresies*, Book V, preface).

The early fathers stress that we become by grace what Christ is by nature. St Gregory of Nyssa takes this to mean that we are raised beyond the limitations of our human nature. This began with the raising of Christ's human nature beyond its limits, in which we will partake endlessly as members of the Body of Christ (*The Life of Moses*). St Athanasius wrote, "God became man so that man might become god" (*On the Incarnation* 54:3). What would appear impossible, that fallen humanity might become holy as God is holy, becomes possible through Jesus Christ.

We need to dispel a number of false ideas that circulate about theosis.

We do not become God. That is impossible. There is a great gulf fixed between humanity and God, fixed by our estrangement from God, fixed by God's holiness (otherness), fixed by our nature as created beings. We do not become little gods, each of us with our own planet, or because our nature is to be "gods" (as some American or Eastern religions teach). We do not participate in God's *essence* (*ousia* is the Greek term). The church had to make this distinction early on, to salvage the concept from the erroneous notion that we actually become God. God forces no one to become good, or to re-enter communion with Him; we are creatures of free will and must choose to enter the process. This alignment is called *synergeia* – our working together with the Holy Spirit. Lastly, theosis does not mean emotional mystical experiences, undefined spirituality, or the loose mysticism so easily talked about in our culture. Theosis is a solidly Christian experience. It was shared in the early church both East and West, and surely was part of the Celtic Christian experience.

Theosis means that we participate in God's *energies*. *Energeia* is the Greek term, and it means a working, but always of a divine sort. This participation begins with repentance and forgiveness. We become "godly," to use an old Protestant term. By participating in God's energies, we align with God's will and purpose in the world. We participate in the sacraments and in spiritual practices like fasting and charitable work, and so participate in Christ. We enter into struggle against the temptations to conform to the image of Christ. Lastly, as we contemplate God, we come to know what it means to be fully human. St Irenaeus said it so well: "the glory of God is a human being fully revealed" (*Against Heresies*, Book V).

Pascha, or Easter, is the model for this whole experience; at Pascha we "come, receive the Light" which shines forth from the resurrection. Theosis is, in fact, the reconciliation of the created order (man, the universe) with the uncreated (God).

We experience growth in Christ in spurts. Sometimes we experience reversals, as when we are trapped by our temptations and cannot seem to get out from under them. The promise of the Christian life, however, is that we shall "see (God) face to face." In the meantime, let us move toward the warmth and the light of God's countenance.

FURTHER RECOMMENDED READING

Background on the Desert Saints

Brock, Sebastian P., and Susan Ashbrook Harvey. *Holy Women of the Syrian Orient*. Berkeley: University of California Press, 1998.

Chrysostomos, Archimandrite. *The Ancient Fathers of the Desert*. Brookline, MA: Hellenic College Press, 1980.

Chryssavgis, John. *In the Heart of the Desert: The Spirituality of the Desert Fathers and Mothers*. Bloomington IN: Word Wisdom, 2003.

Cowan, James. *Desert Father: A Journey in the Wilderness with Saint Anthony*. Boston: Shambhala Press, 2004.

Merton, Thomas. *The Wisdom of the Desert*. New York: New Dimension, 1960.

Swan, Laura. *The Forgotten Desert Mothers*. New York: Paulist Press, 2001.

Waddell, Helen. *The Desert Fathers*. New York: Random House Vintage Edition, 1998.

Ward, Sr Benedicta, SLG. *The Wisdom of the Desert Fathers*. Fairacres, Oxford: SLG Press, 1975.

The Celts

Chadwick, Nora. *Celtic Britain*. New York: Praeger, 1963 (entire text online).

————. *The Celts*. London: Penguin, 1991.

Cunliffe, Barry. *The Celtic World*. New York: McGraw-Hill, 1979.

Duffy, Kevin. *Who Were the Celts?* New York: Fall River Press, 1996.

Ellis, Peter Berresford. *The Celtic Empire, The First Millennium of Celtic History 100 BC - 51 AD*. Chapel Hill: Carolina Academic Press, 1960.

Raftery, Joseph, ed., *The Celts*. Cork: Mercier Press, 1967.

History and Theology

Bede, The Venerable. *Ecclesiastical History of the English People*. Ed. D. H. Farmer. London: Penguin Classics, 1991.

Cahill, Thomas. *How the Irish Saved Civilization*. New York: Doubleday, 1995.

Cartwright, Jane. *Feminine Sanctity and Spirituality in Medieval Wales*. Cardiff: University of Wales Press, 2008

Duncan, Anthony. *The Elements of Celtic Christianity*. Shaftesbury, Dorset: Element Books, 1992.

Hunter, George G., III. *The Celtic Way of Evangelism*. Nashville: Abingdon Press, 2000.

Joyce, Timothy. *Celtic Christianity: A Sacred Tradition, A Vision of Hope*. Maryknoll NY: Orbis Books, 1998.

McNeill, John T. and Helen Gamer. *The Medieval Penitentials*. New York: Columbia University Press, 1938.

Moorhouse, Geoffrey. *Sun Dancing: A Vision of Medieval Ireland*. New York: Harcourt Brace and Company, 1997.

Newell, J. Philip. *Christ of the Celts: The Healing of Creation.* San Francisco: Jossey-Bass, 2008.

Van de Weyer, Robert. *Celtic Gifts: Orders of Ministry in the Celtic Church.* Norwich: Canterbury Press, 1997.

Walsh, John R. and Thomas Bradley. *A History of the Irish Church 400-700 AD.* Dublin: The Columba Press, 1991.

Books on Celtic Prayer

Adam, David. *The Edge of Glory: Prayers in the Celtic Tradition.* Harrisburg: Morehouse, 1985.

———. *The Open Gate: Celtic Prayers for Growing Spiritually.* Harrisburg: Morehouse, 1995.

———. *The Rhythm of Life: Celtic Daily Prayer.* Harrisburg: Morehouse, 1996.

Carmichael, Alexander. *Carmina Gadelica.* Edinburgh: T & A Constable, 1900. [online]. Available at http://www.sacred-texts.com/neu/celt/cg1/cg1000.htm.

De Waal, Esther. *Every Earthly Blessing: Rediscovering the Celtic Tradition.* Harrisburg: Morehouse, 1999.

———. *God under My Roof: Celtic Songs and Blessings.* Brewster MA: Paraclete Press, 1997.

Newell, J. Philip. *Celtic Prayers from Iona.* New York: Paulist Press, 1997.

The Northumbria Community, introduction by Richard J. Foster. *Celtic Daily Prayer.* San Francisco: Harper, 2002.

Simpson, Ray. *Celtic Blessings: Prayers for Everyday Life.* Chicago: Loyola Press, 1999.

———. *Celtic Worship through the Year.* London: Hodder & Stoughton, 1998.

Celtic Art

Backhouse, Janet. *The Lindisfarne Gospels.* London: The British Library, n.d.

Bain, George. *Celtic Art: The Methods of Construction.* New York: Dover Press, 1973.

Bain, Iain. *Celtic Knotwork.* New York: Sterling Publishing, 1997.

Cirker, Blanche, ed. *The Book of Kells: Selected Plates.* New York: Dover, 1982.

Davies, Damian Walford and Anne Eastham. *Saints and Stones.* Llandysul: Gomer Press, 2002.

Lord, Peter, with research assistant John Morgan-Guy. *The Visual Culture of Wales: Medieval Vision.* Cardiff: University of Wales Press, 2003.

Meehan, Bernard. *The Book of Durrow.* Dublin: Roberts Rinehart Publishers, 1996.

Redknap, Mark. *The Christian Celts: Treasures of Late Celtic Wales.* Cardiff: National Museum of Wales, 1991.

Richardson, Hilary, and John Scarry. *An Introduction to Irish High Crosses.* Dublin: Mercier Press, 1990.

Sykes, Homer. *Mysterious Britain.* London: Weidenfeld and Nicolson, 1993.

Celtic Spirituality

Allchin, A M. *God's Presence Makes the World: The Celtic Vision through the Centuries in Wales.* London: Darton, Longman and Todd, 1997.

———. *Praise above All: Discovering the Welsh Tradition.* Cardiff: University of Wales Press, 1991.

———. *Resurrection's Children: Exploring the Way towards God*. Norwich: Canterbury Press, 1998.

———. *The World is a Wedding: Explorations in Christian Spirituality*. New York: Oxford, 1978.

Buckley, Maria. *Celtic Spirituality*. Cork: Mercier Press, 2001.

Davies, Oliver. *Celtic Christianity in Early Medieval Wales*. Cardiff: University of Wales Press, 1996.

Davies, Oliver, in collaboration with Thomas O'Loughlin. *Celtic Spirituality*. New York: Paulist Press, 1999. (the definitive guide)

Jones, John Miriam, S. C. *With An Eagle's Eye: a Seven-Day Sojourn in Celtic Spirituality*. Notre Dame IN: Ave Maria Press, 1998.

Newell, J. Philip. *Listening for the Heartbeat of God: A Celtic Spirituality*. New York: Paulist Press, 1997.

———. *One Foot in Eden: A Celtic View of the Stages of Life*. New York: Paulist Press, 1999.

———. *The Book of Creation: An Introduction to Celtic Spirituality*. New York: Paulist Press, 1999.

O Riordain, John J O. *Irish Catholic Spirituality: Celtic and Roman*. Dublin: Columba Press, 1998.

———. *The Music of What Happens*. Dublin: Columba Press, 1996.

Sheldrake, Philip. *Living Between Worlds: Place and Journey in Celtic Spirituality*. London: Darton, Longman and Todd, 1995.

Thomas, Patrick. *A Candle in the Darkness: Celtic Spirituality from Wales*. Llandysul: Gomer Press, 1993.

Saints

Adam, David. *The Cry of the Deer: Meditations on the Hymn of St Patrick.* Harrisburg: Morehouse, 1987.

———. *A Desert in The Ocean: The Spiritual Journey According to St Brendan the Navigator.* New York: Paulist Press, 2000.

———. *Flame in My Heart: St Aidan for Today.* Harrisburg: Morehouse, 1998.

Bury, J. B., edited by Jon M. Sweeney. *Ireland's Saint: The Essential Biography of St. Patrick.* Brewster MA: Paraclete Press, 2008.

Cartwright, Jane. *Feminine Sanctity and Spirituality in Medieval Wales.* Cardiff: University of Wales Press, 2008.

Mitton, Michael. *The Soul of Celtic Spirituality in the Lives of Its Saints.* Mystic CT: Twenty-third Publications, 1996.

Pennick, Nigel. *The Celtic Saints.* New York: Sterling Publishing, 1997.

Pitkin Guides. *Celtic Saints.* Hampshire: Jarrold Publishing, 2003.

Sellner, Edward C. *Wisdom of the Celtic Saints.* Notre Dame IN: Ave Maria Press, 1993.

———. *Stories of the Celtic Soul Friends: Their Meaning for Today.* New York: Paulist Press, 2004.

Simms, George Otto. *Brendan the Navigator.* Dublin: O'Brien Press, 1989. (children's book)

Skinner, John, trans. *The Confession of St. Patrick.* New York: Doubleday Image, 1998.

Whiteside, Lesley. *The Spirituality of St. Patrick.* Dublin: Columba Press, 1996.

SOURCES AND NOTES

"Guide Me O Thou Great Redeemer" Welsh and English texts are in public domain.

Tropars associated with the lead essay on each saint: These ancient prayers in the Orthodox tradition are, to the best of our knowledge, in public domain.

All scripture quotations are from the Revised Standard Version. New York: Thomas Nelson and Sons, 1952; the King James Version, or the author's own translations.

The title *A Staff to the Pilgrim* is from *Carmina Gadelica*, Volume I, "The Invocation of the Graces," pp. 7ff. The full text of the stanza is:

> *A shade art thou in the heat,*
> *A shelter art thou in the cold,*
> *Eyes art thou to the blind,*
> *A staff art thou to the pilgrim,*
> *An island art thou at sea,*
> *A fortress art thou on land,*
> *A well art thou in the desert,*
> *Health art thou to the ailing.*

3. Solitude

The Archibald MacLeish quote is from *Poetry and Experience.* Baltimore: Penguin Press, 1964.

4. Stones

The Henri Nouwen quote is from *Out of Solitude: Three Meditations on the Christian Life.* Notre Dame IN: Ave Maria Press, 2004.

The J. Philip Newell quote is from *Christ of the Celts: The Healing of Creation.* San Francisco: Jossey-Bass, 2008, p. 52.

The *Black Book of Carmarthen* quote is available online at: *Celtic Literature Collective and Jones's Celtic Encyclopedia*: http://www.maryjones.us/ctexts/bbc11.html.

5. Spirit

The Stephen Mitchell quotes are from *The Second Book of the Tao.* New York: Penguin Books, 2010.

The Mary Oliver quote is from her poem "Snow Geese," from the collection *Why I Wake Early: New Poems.* Boston: Beacon Press, 2004, p. 34.

The Tatiana Goricheva quote is from *Talking about God is Dangerous.* New York: Crossroad Publishing Co., 1989, p. 91.

6. Supplication

The David Jones quote is from *Epoch & Artist.* London: Faber and Faber, 1952, p. 28.

The Dylan Thomas quote is from *Collected Poems.* New York: New Directions, 1952, p. v.

7. Spiritual Friendship

The Henri Nouwen quote is from *The Inner Voice of Love.* New York: Image Books reprint, 1999.

8. Sent

The George Hunter quote is from *The Celtic Way of Evangelism.* Nashville: Abingdon Press, 2000, p. 26.

The St. Augustine quote is from *On Christian Doctrine, Book I.* Available online at: http://courses.missouristate.edu/markgiven/rel580/doctrine.pdf.

The Czeslaw Milosz quote is from *The Witness of Poetry.* Cambridge: Harvard University Press, 1983, p. 10.

ABOUT THE AUTHOR

Fr Gabriel Cooper Rochelle, MA, MDiv, ThM, PhD, is an Orthodox priest. A cleric for over 50 years, he enjoys birding, baking bread, bicycling, and calligraphy in his spare time. Giving readers the benefit of his half-century in ministry, he writes on many subjects, with Celtic Christian spirituality being one of his favorite topics. Fr Gabriel and his wife live in Las Cruces, New Mexico.

If you would like to correspond with Fr Gabriel, learn more about Celtic Christian spirituality, or receive a complimentary set of the drawings in this book (suitable for coloring), please go to: www.frgabrielrochelle.com/a-staff-to-the-pilgrim or www.goldenalleypress.com/fr-gabriel-rochelle

Printed in Great Britain
by Amazon